Bright BLUE

Bright BLUE

Rabbi Lionel Blue's Thoughts for the Day

British Broadcasting Corporation

Published by the
British Broadcasting Corporation
35 Marylebone High Street
London W1M 4AA

First published 1985
ISBN 0 563 20395 1
© Lionel Blue 1985

Contents

Introduction

When I was asked if I would collect these talks for publication, I smiled politely and said, 'Yes, of course.' I then rushed home and made a frantic hunt through kitchen cupbords and spare room wardrobes to see what I could rescue. I had jotted them down in trains, in hospital waiting-rooms, sitting up in bed, or prone in my bath. Some were written on the backs of envelopes. A few had wandered into a book of low calorie cooking, and the one on suffering was a doorstop.

On reassembling them and reading them through, I was pleased at their frankness. My only regret was that I hadn't been franker. I am not a courageous person but I am a busy one, and inner truth comes quicker than artifice. I just didn't have time to put on the style, or be a spokesman for anybody or anything.

I like the radio (I still think of it as the wireless), and my transistor is as close to me as my Bible (being honest, even closer). It helps me leap through the hoop of morning anxiety like a performing seal, and after I say my prayers at night I nestle against it under my duvet. It has replaced the teddy of my childhood. Only God and my dog have given me more companionship. So I enjoy chatting over the radio as well as listening to it.

I get engrossed in the letters I receive and I'm sorry I answer them so slowly. But I have to write them all by hand, and some of the questions need more than a yes or no answer, like: Dear Rabbi (occasionally Rabbit which I rather like) Blue/Glue/or Bloom, Tell me briefly all the difference between Jews and Christians. PS. Why aren't you a Christian? One day I should like to retreat to a quiet place like a Jewish College or a monastery for a month (or a lifetime) to write out a proper answer to that one.

I put in the jokes, because I've had a difficult time lately, and I needed to cheer myself up. Also 'Religion' in a worldly sense can't help being rather funny – all that dressing up! The logic which connects all the pieces in this book, the sacred and the profane, is as wayward as Proust's, but not so refined. But it is my own. Little bits of music take me back to butties in Blackpool, not to musing on Musset (the one who 'called his cat Pusset').

I like dedicating books but there is a limit to the number of dedicatees you are allowed to include. So let's see how many I can get away with: to Janny whose price is beyond rubies, to my mother who prefers diamonds, to Father Gordian who allows me to use him, not because he is naïve but because he is Christian, to Kim my good companion for 18 years, to Jim who gave me the courage to rebuild a home, to Eva, who trusts in God and survives.

And an especial thank you to God, Whom I fell in love with when I was a student, and Who has stuck with me, and to my friends on the 'Today' programme, who are the only people I've ever enjoyed talking to before breakfast – apart from God of course.

ONE

The Memory Trap

I am a Jew, and I am glued to my religion by memory. Theologies change, and beliefs can die, but never memory. I expel it from the front door of my mind and it steals in through the back door of my dreams and prayers.

When I returned to London after the Second World War, I knew my soul would have to live on memory and little else in the years ahead, for everything had gone. There was a bomb hole where my house had been, the synagogues of the East End were boarded up, and the great edifice of Jewish lore and tradition had crumbled away.

I looked for an old man in the market. In a thin, cracked voice he used to sing the songs of Zion, accompanied by old, cracked records on a wind-up machine: songs about piety and potatoes and poverty; songs about marriage-brokers and beadles, railing against the self-importance of rabbis; ironic, passionate songs about the Holy One, Blessed be He, and the terrible sufferings He imposed upon His people. The old man was no longer there, and his songs had died with him. No one remembered his biting words; sentiment had already been at work and softened them.

Even Yiddish, the language of my memories, had gone. People told me a great poet slept now on park benches, for his audience had been burnt back into the dust and ashes from which they came. Dust covered the old notice boards of the Yiddish cinemas, and the Yiddish slogans on the walls of old synagogues. The marriage-brokers with their red umbrellas had gone, and who could find a wonder-working rabbi any more with a skill for amulets? (Some of them worked.) Who could find old people to recite the Book of Psalms before funerals? There were no factory workers who studied the scriptures at five in the morning before breakfast and drudgery.

Since my childhood I have lived in many worlds – the tight and tidy world of middle-class suburbs, the loose, bohemian worlds of Amsterdam and Paris, the lost worlds of contemplation, worlds ecclesiastical and economical with their committees and back-slapping and over-strong Martinis. But even as I sip from my glass, I know they are not as real as the world of my memory. My home died but it remains my home. Since then I have lived in houses.

Many Jewish people feel this. We meet in Brussels, successful Common Market folk. Our party goes with a swing, until someone says, 'You know how it used to be', or a record of 'My Yiddishe Momme' is played for a laugh. Then the past in all its force overwhelms us. All that is western and successful is torn away from us. We have gone back a hundred years in time, and across half a continent in space. I am grateful to memory for it.

Memory helped me back to belief, and memory tried to strangle its growth. Memory has been my salvation, and memory has been my prison. My soul cannot survive without it, but my spirit cannot journey forwards encumbered with it. So it is with all believers, for we suffer from nostalgia. We yearn for a Yiddish world that died, for the purity of the early Christians, or 'old-time' religion, for an empire that was lost, or a revolution that was betrayed.

Newspapers, like scriptures, urge us to remember. Never forget Hiroshima, they say, or the Holocaust. But I do not always want to. A long time ago I based my religion on memory and its traditions. Now I need to rebuild it to keep faith with the needs of the present and the future, not just the past. Memory can be a trap – it is too easy.

TWO

The Voice from the Juke-box

I went into religion partly because I was not very good at dealing with the world. I thought this was my unworldliness, but it was in fact my fear and incompetence. In my innocence I confused spirituality with droopiness, and I imagined myself with equally droopy colleagues, sighing blessings to each other.

I got a rude shock. Synagogue (and church) general meetings are not the Communion of Saints, and an awful lot of religious business is concerned with balance sheets, not blessings. At international meetings, where the pace is hotter, I got used to seeing clerics fingering calculators as expertly as their beads. You have to be very competent to keep the show on the road – and I don't mean any disrespect.

This led to a crisis in my religious life. My religious organisation was a place where I gave blessings; this was after all what I was paid to do. But it was not a place where I seemed to receive any – at least not obviously. As my teacher tartly remarked when I complained to him, the congregation employed me to solve their problems. I didn't pay them to solve mine.

Blessings did come to me, but not from the place I had expected. They flowed into me from the worldly world I had rejected. A major source of ideas for sermons and spirituality came to me in airport lounges, bars, cafés (not always the genteel ones) and bus queues. To my astonishment the still, small voice of God spoke to me through the clamour of a juke-box.

I remember a song of Marlene Dietrich: 'Where Have All the Flowers Gone?' she sang. Young girls had picked them. They had given them to their men. The men had gone to war, and got killed. Out of their graves little flowers grew. Where had they gone, those flowers? Well, young girls had picked them. *Und so weiter . . . Und so weiter . . .* Etc. . . . Etc. . . .

In a café in Germany I looked up and saw a young girl and a boy at the next table. A vase of flowers separated them. The full tragedy of Europe came home to me, and I knew the work I must do. So many people had to be reconciled to break that terrible repetition. God had spoken.

THREE

A Rabbi's Job

Jews are supposed to recite three services a day, and if possible say a hundred blessings, though I'm not sure whether this is inclusive or exclusive of those in the services. This is their duty, or so the rabbis tell us, and many Jews, like many religious people these days, don't fulfil their duty to the letter.

I fulfil mine more often than many, not only for exalted reasons but because religion happens to be my job and my livelihood. I do not know if the Almighty gets much benefit out of my duty prayers, but I do, and so presumably do the congregations I have served because both of us turn up to the synagogue on time. What benefit they confer is a bit of a puzzle. These duty prayers save me from having to make up my own religion, which would be tiring, and probably impossible. I once thought I could improve on the existing varieties; now I don't.

When I was a rabbinic student, I tried to say every word of my duty prayers with love and intention, lingering over every sacred syllable, waiting coyly in the vestry until I was towed in, afloat with sufficient uplift. The service became too long, one lady burnt her lunch, and quite a few broke their appointments. My meditative voice also sent everybody to sleep.

I now prepare for duty prayers at duty services by realising that reciting them is not a love affair nor a privilege, it is a duty – possibly to God but certainly to my congregation, who have employed me for that purpose. A part of religion is business, and I would like it to be honest business. Part of my preparation for communal prayer consists in making sure that everything works well, that the prayer books are out, that the Ark is unlocked, that the eternal flame is not going to flicker out on me, or get switched off, and that I get the announcements right.

It doesn't seem very exalted, but that's what duty is – not jam, not cake, but daily bread, and this stale bread is what the world lives on. I prefer to say duty prayers with love and without temper, but with temper or love I have to give fair value.

Some rabbis thought that religion was 'the destruction of the ego'. And routine prayers are as good as any for filing away the ego's bumps. Their very routine-ness shows you that you are not the centre of the universe – it isn't there to jump to your tempo: you are there to serve it.

So now I stand in the vestry, checking in my mind that everything is right, not for me but for my community. My only prayer is an ejaculatory one: 'O my God – only three minutes and I'm on!'

FOUR

Thy Servant – a Dog

I was in love with my dog Re'ach and wanted to see the world as she saw it. So in the office of my synagogue I went down on all fours and half closed my eyes, because sight is not so important for dogs. I dilated my nostrils as I wanted to smell my way into her reality. I lurched around the room trying to concentrate on bones, watched by my dog Re'ach herself, who sat on her haunches, tensely calculating

what was in it for her. I was also being watched by an important member of my community, who had come into the room unnoticed.

He looked at me, I looked at him, and my courage failed. 'I'm mousing,' I said brazenly. It was the first thought that came to mind. 'Looking for a mouse,' I added helpfully. He has treated me since politely but distantly.

But never mind, I did get some inkling into her doggy mind. At services she stood up and sat down like other worshippers when it suited her, and this gave her an undeserved reputation for piety. I think she was just a bourgeois conformist myself. Still, that's the way a lot of people get religious reputations.

Was she religious? Well, she had a flair for liturgy, as I've said, but prayer I doubt. I don't think she was capable of believing in a being that didn't smell.

Was she a Jewish dog? I think not. Like most conformists, ecclesiastical or otherwise, she disliked jokes about things that mattered to her – bones, or chocolate drops, or sex, or her plastic chop that squeaked. She had no feeling for the absurd or the ridiculous, and for Jews there is a ridiculous side to everything that matters, however profound.

I get a lot out of taking services, for example, but what does God make of me, prancing and bobbing up and down like a demented thing in bits of bombazine and white sheeting? How does my Father in heaven regard the set prayers I offer up, in which I alternately butter Him up and then nag Him, in fact just like I buttered up my parents on earth. In any case I am finite and He is infinite. I have as much chance of understanding Him as has a cow trying to program a computer.

I can cope with all this absurdity for two reasons. Though I don't understand God's reality, in practice I experience it. And if you put half as much effort into prayer as you do into a driving test, or learning to play the guitar or holiday Spanish, you could experience it too. It's that simple. Secondly, the absurdities and tragedies which no theology can comprehend can be assimilated in jokes.

I like the story of a Jewish woman who fainted in a theatre, crying, 'Get me a doctor.' As the doctor bent over her she beamed up at him: 'Have I got a girl for you!'

Or the Jewish lady who gazed at an opulent funeral and said with a sigh, 'Now that's what I call living!'

My dog Re'ach was a thing of beauty, but, alas, a 'goy' – a non-Jew – for ever. She was a serious dog who took serious things seriously. She would have dismissed such jokes and frivolities with a contemptuous bark and a dismissive wave of her paw. 'Let us return,' she would say, 'to things that matter – to my plastic chop that squeaks.'

FIVE
That's Life

When I was in Amsterdam I had two friends. One of them was young and suffering from life – as we all do. But Life – with a capital L – is particularly acute and painful in the teens and early twenties. The other was older and had transferred his preoccupation from Life to stamp collecting, which is much easier on the nerves. The young one shook his head despondently. 'My parents never understood me,' he groaned. 'They were,' he whispered, 'bourgeois!' The other lifted his head from his stamps and said amiably, 'Don't take it too heavy, dear, don't take it too heavy.'

I suggest we take this remark as our basic text in the coming years, for from what the experts say our future may be quite dreadful – if it even exists. It is, after all, possible that we have blundered into a nuclear chain reaction of events which might blow us all into kingdom come. But whether we have or we haven't, we are going to require all the lightness and humour we can muster to accomplish the great religious miracle and transform our bad temper into a little kindness and a little trust.

To prepare myself for such realities I decided to educate myself politically. A friend of mine had come by the complete works of Kim Il Sung, the North Korean Marxist leader, and I have made an assault on them. They are very solid. But in my student days I did a commando course on the many volumes of the Talmud and this stands me in good stead. I have virtuously attempted the first volume of my political education, but I am already running out of steam. It is so serious, with no jokes and no pictures, and 'What use is a book without pictures?' as Alice so rightly remarked – and she should have included jokes. For only when a person can laugh at himself is he saved from his own self-importance. And only when a religion or an ideology can laugh at itself is it redeemed from its own fanaticism, although it finds this as difficult as an elephant dancing a pirouette.

In the tragic history of Judaism there is a well of bubbling laughter which is both human and humane and even softens up the sternness of the scriptures. Here is an example. It is about the Talmud, that weighty and learned source of Jewish religious law.

A Gentile came to a rabbi and said, 'Rabbi, teach me Talmud.'

The rabbi gazed at him sorrowfully and said, 'Go away. Gentiles can't learn Talmud. They just haven't got the head for it – it's not their fault.'

'Try me, try me,' said the student urgently.

'Well,' said the rabbi, 'I'll give you a simple Talmudic problem, though it's no use, but see what you can do with it.' He started to chant, 'If two men come down a chimney, and one comes out dirty and the other comes out clean, who goes to wash first?'

'Oh, that's easy,' was the reply, 'the dirty one.'

The rabbi shook his head sadly. 'I told you it wouldn't work.'

'But what's wrong?' exclaimed the bewildered student.

'Look,' said the rabbi, 'the dirty one looks at the clean one and says if he's clean, then I must be clean, so he stays where he is. The clean one looks at the dirty one and says if he's dirty, then I must be dirty, so he goes to wash first. You just haven't got the head for it, that's all.'

'Please, please,' said the student. 'Just give me one more chance.'

'All right,' said the rabbi, 'though I warn you, God didn't make you that way. But listen carefully.' He chanted again, 'If two men come down a chimney and one comes out dirty and the other comes out clean, who goes to wash first?'

'Ah,' said the student triumphantly, 'I know, the clean one!'

'Fool,' said the rabbi, 'whoever heard of two men coming down a chimney and one coming out dirty and the other coming out clean? I told you it's no use.'

Because such jokes reveal and deflate, they can exasperate you or enrage you, and if they do, well, that's life. And if this exasperates you even more, remember the words of my friend, which have become our text – don't take it too heavy, dear, don't take it too heavy!

SIX

The Nazi and the Bicycle Riders

The Nazi said to the Jew, 'The Jews are responsible for all Germany's problems.'

'Yes,' said the Jew, 'the Jews and the bicycle riders.'

'Why the bicycle riders?' said the Nazi, puzzled.

'Why the Jews?' said the Jew.

It's easy to make a devil out of anyone who stands in our way or who has a different opinion from our own. At Christmas and public holidays there is usually a lull in devil-making but it soon starts up again – just wait until the goodwill evaporates. The lazy Left will do it with classes, the lazy Right will do it with races. Government and opposition politicians will make devils out of each other, though we know it's a game – but a foolhardy one. And I shall do it, too. I shall make a devil out of the woman in front of me at the ticket office, who is buying a season ticket in the rush hour. I shall hate people on strike who spoil my holiday. I shall hate people whose success I fancy should be mine. Whenever I feel this way, I add to the present object of my hate the words 'and the bicycle riders', and then I realise how absurd it is.

What is the devil, after all? Just my own weakness, my own lack of courage, the problem I can't face, the bit of my own self I can't love. We are our own devils. I used to fight my devils in prayer, but now I send them up in jokes.

SEVEN

Putting My Foot in It

I fell into a grave once. I was burying an old lady in winter, and the ground was icy. I stood around the grave with the mourners. They passed me a spade to throw in some earth, for this is part of the Jewish ritual. In my fervour I got carried away, and slipped – the earth went in first, then went the spade, and then me.

I was very angry. I felt such an awful fool, such a ninny. On the way down I prayed. I prayed that the

mourners had not been stingy over the coffin, and had bought one with a lid made of solid oak, not one made out of plywood. She was a dignified old lady, and unlike Tristan and Isolde, neither of us would have appreciated reunification in death.

Climbing out of a grave is not easy, or dignified. I am not athletic, and I was tangled up in my ample robes of black bombazine and my velvet hat. They passed down ropes, but it was as difficult as a ski-lift, and I kept on falling and bouncing back on that awful coffin lid. I peered up at the mourners and they peered down at me, and at last I knew what it was like to be at the receiving end of a funeral.

A muscular grave-digger finally hauled me out, and I sat on the edge of the grave, while the mourners fed me from a brandy flask which had appeared as spontaneously as miracles should, but rarely do.

Later, in a café, I thought about what had happened, and felt thoroughly ashamed of my prayer. Jonah had fallen into a whale, but at least he had prayed a sort of psalm. I should have thought of eternity too, for the circumstances were propitious, but all I had thought about was my own dignity and a coffin lid. In life, I knew I would fall into many dark holes; would my religion never rise or sink to the occasion? I knew that God was in such moments of bliss as I had experienced. But where was such grandeur in a slapstick comedy, in absurdity, in farce? There are not many jokes in sacred scripture, and congregations get uneasy if they have to giggle. One unexpected laugh can collapse the grandest liturgy. Yet for most of us our problems are neither tragic nor comic. They are not the results of our great vices or virtues, they are just consequences of our silliness.

So, as I sipped the coffee, I took a look at my self-importance, and my inflated ecclesiastical pride. And I did not like them at all. So I put down the cup and prayed to God.

'Lord, at least help me enjoy my own absurdity and not to take my silliness too seriously.' And this prayer He has granted me more than most.

EIGHT

Look at the Birdie!

Religious institutions often treat the Holy Spirit like a budgie. They coo at him, and want him to answer 'tweet-tweet'. They would like him to fly out of his cage and into their lives, just for a minute or two of course. But this bird won't move – he just seems to eye them distantly, birdily and beadily.

Then they say, 'He is an ungrateful beggar. Doesn't he realise there is a recession on, and lots of birds are homeless? Look at them all migrating to the North Pole or the Sahara, while birdie here has a nice ecclesiastical cage and central heating.'

I don't think the Spirit is like a budgie or even a dove, as he is usually depicted. He is a very strange bird indeed and wilier than we thought. He is, in fact, much like God on Mount Sinai. 'I will be gracious to whom I will be gracious, and show mercy to whom I will show mercy.' Beat that for wilfulness.

But when the bird has flown, how do we get him back into our lives? For this bird means freedom and soaring, and without his wings there is no life in the universe, no heady love. Getting the Spirit back into our lives is like luring a rare bird into our gardens.

Firstly, be quite clear that you are not going to cage him, because caging free creatures is nasty, and in this case quite useless. But put on protective clothing, because the Spirit can lead you into strange places, to condemned prisoners in their cells, and into the wilderness. He has done that before, you know.

You can, of course, put out little pious titbits for

him, juicy prayers that you have cooked up on your own. But he is so capricious. You never know what he is going to accept. It was said, 'The wind bloweth where it listeth . . . but thou canst not tell whence it cometh and whither it goeth: so is every one that is born of the Spirit.' Too true, too true, so blow you and your bribes.

There is only one way to get him that I know, and that is to stalk him – but very gently. This is how you do it. Pretend to be like him, imitate his ways, and all you know of his habits. Pretend you are flying. Don't just be ethical, be good! Do foolish and generous things for people. Don't hit them with your clumsy old fists! Touch them as softly and gently as if you had the wings of a dove – not those great hairy arms.

If you are that gentle, birdie gets interested and confused, you know. He thinks perhaps you aren't the clumsy ape you seem, but a soaring, gentle, wild bird, like himself. If you want to have the Spirit, pray to be like the Spirit, pray that you are so like the Spirit that no one, not even the Spirit, can tell you apart.

'Coo-oo, tweet-tweet. Good luck!'

NINE

Take Care – Take Care!

Life's a tricky old thing and getting trickier all the time. There is a substitute for everything now, and the picture on the package tells you more about you and what you want to believe than the contents. You can be a martyr, for example, without discomfort, or a revolutionary just for the kicks, or you can disguise your private hates with social concern.

You can imitate the Spirit too. With practice you can fool people with your imitation of it. You can even fool yourself if that's what you want. But you won't

fool the Spirit. That dove is a wise old bird, with that knowing look you find in untamed creatures.

Take gentleness, for example. There has been an awful lot of it around since the hippies moved in from California, and flower power people pressed dying daisies into your hand in Oxford Street. The kindness was clinging, but sticky like chewing gum, and you couldn't get away from it. Even in pubs your own mates didn't give you a hearty farewell. They looked into your eyes, the rats, sadly and soulfully, and gently said, 'Bless you, take care!' on a rising note.

Now you can be gentle not because the Spirit moves you, but because you are so bloody feeble you can't be anything else. It's easier to agree with everybody, even if they are wrong, than to disagree with them because you are right. So you say, 'Yes, yes, yes', and everybody exclaims, 'What a gentle creature you are, so strong in the Spirit you know.' Of course they don't mean it, but neither did you, so why complain?

You can also be gentle because you have a taste for emotional blackmail, and gentle weakness is strong stuff, if used cleverly.

You can also be really gentle, and hopelessly wrong, if you lack discrimination. If, for example, you are

...tle to the wrong person, and hard on the right one. In this case the wrong person is usually yourself, and the right person someone else.

But sometimes you meet the real thing, that gentleness which is the fruit of the Spirit, and very disconcerting it is. It is quite ruthless, as love usually is. It is so uncalculating that you don't know where to put it or how to respond to it, so it makes you quite cross. It is so spontaneous and direct that there is no time to protect yourself with psychology or theology. It is so convincing that you know it can't be just natural, but something more – supernatural.

So instinctively you look up. And there's that crazy dove circling around overhead. 'Lord, make it descend on us!'

TEN

Odd Man Out

My old teacher, Leo Baeck, was an odd man who became the Chief Rabbi of Germany in 1933, of all times. He actually returned to Germany from America just as the Second World War started, and he was also one of the first to visit Germany after the war had ended, despite his years in a concentration camp. In the camp he gave secret lectures at night on the Hellenic influence on Judaism. He disliked wasting time, even in hell. Like Bonhoeffer and others, he knew that being religious meant being involved in the reconciliation business.

It was because of him that I blundered into the field of German-Jewish relations, and then into the field of Jewish-Moslem relations. The latter have been getting steadily worse since the First World War, and Jews and Moslems scarcely know each other now, and don't meet. When they do, they talk *at* each other, not *to* each other. Mrs Cohen does not have tea with Mrs Muhammed, and there is no established friendship society with eminent patrons, like the one which links Jews and Christians.

Anyway, this is how it happened. A German pastor who had run an underground church in the war invited some religious Jews, Christians and Moslems to meet. We met in Berlin because the bishop there gave us some money when no one else bothered. Hardly any Jews or Christians were aware of the new Islamic diaspora which was taking root in Europe, or could see the makeshift minarets sprouting out of the industrial wasteland in the west.

The meeting-place was a pleasant old house, but its beautiful location knocked the Jews sideways. Unintentionally, it happened to be only a few doors away from the house where the final liquidation of the Jews had been planned. The timing was also disastrous. Again unintentionally, we found ourselves meeting for the first time during the Arab-Israeli war of 1967.

None of us knew each other or who we were or what we represented. I am a Convener of a Jewish Ecclesiastical Court, called a Reform Jewish Beth Din. Unless you inhabit my particular ghetto I doubt if this will enlighten you. I also had no idea what an Imam was or a Qadi or a Sheikh – what he did, and where he did it. The sources of confusion were endless, and sometimes very funny. Catholics and Protestants disagreed about Karl Barth while the Middle East burnt, and I sat up through the night with a Moslem trying to translate this strange theology into the legal religious language we both use.

At a reception in our honour we got well-intentioned hospitality and treatment, but westerners do not realise that eastern religions place as much importance on food as on sex. Lumps of pork were solicitously served to Jews, and glasses of hock were politely pressed on Moslems. Both suspected a plot.

Talking to someone seems simple, but it wasn't simple for us. We found it easier to address the Almighty or perorate the Muse of History than to have a simple chat with each other. Christians ran after Jews, Jews ran after Moslems, and Moslems ran after Christians. I'd never realised that to make real contact with someone you had to see them as they saw themselves, and not as your own reflection. How much faith one needed for real conversation.

To listen required even more. When a person or a group examines their own failings, they normally only recognise a few foibles. Five minutes' real listening to a trusted outsider can be more shattering than days of meditation. To my surprise I learned that the Moslems were our neighbours, not just in the Middle East, but living alongside Jewish communities in Europe. In the eighties this is a commonplace; in the sixties it was a shock. Like my own grandparents two or three generations ago, the Moslem guest workers were doing the unwanted dirty jobs the establishment refused. (It was before the recession.) For the first time I thought of them, and their life in an unknown country. I thought of Palestinian refugees as well as Jewish ones, and how the world looked if you were not a middle-class Jew like me. Not much of this could be said at the time.

After some years, a Moslem I knew told me some of his real worries and fears about Jews. Any married couple knows how important it is, when you have enough trust to speak the truth, and what courage it requires to do so.

We are just beginning to learn a little from each other. Giving is not difficult, but taking is harder. From my teacher Leo Baeck I learned to try not to be discouraged by political darkness. Religion, after all, teaches that if you accept a darkness and enter it with faith, a door opens and a light appears, that if you do what is right and lean on nothing – the Nothing can support you. A bridge of prayer can extend over a yawning abyss of self-interest, and the feelings behind words are more important than the words themselves.

At the end of the conference a Turk came to the pastor and to me. He said he was really converted to dialogue now, and that both of us should cheer up as we were doing good work. We were really good Moslems at heart, he said, though of course, he added kindly, we weren't aware of it yet.

My rabbinic self considered this startling remark, and I decided it was one of the nicest compliments that anyone had ever paid me.

ELEVEN

The Taste of Redemption

When the children of Israel left Egypt they left in a hurry, like all refugees. There was no time for their bread to rise, so they ate it instead flat and unleavened. It is called the bread of poverty at the Passover meal, and if you are Christian, you probably eat a form of it, too, when you go to communion. You can buy a box of it – it is called matzah – at many supermarkets.

The bread of affliction makes a very tasty breakfast. Dip two sheets in hot water and squeeze them dry. Mix the pieces into three beaten eggs with two pinches of salt and one tablespoon of sugar. Fry the mixture in hot oil until it sets. Put the frying pan under a hot grill and quickly brown the top. Scatter the matzah omelette with sugar and cinnamon and serve in wedges.

At the Passover table foods are not what they seem, and their tastes are deceptive. There is a reminder of the slave labour in ancient Egypt – a memory of the mortar which the slave gangs used, as they suffered and died, building the pyramids of Pharaoh. You can make such mortar yourself. Grate a peeled eating apple and mix it with chopped almonds and hazelnuts, a half teaspoon of cinnamon and some sweet red wine to make a paste. Jewish people put a spoonful of slave labour between two slices of the bread of affliction and eat it before the main course.

After the mortar you drink the tears of the Israelites. You place a hard-boiled egg into the brine and you have a symbol and an *hors d'oeuvre* in one. New life – the egg – comes out of tears. I mash the new life into a salty paste and eat it with the bread of poverty.

Slavery in the ancient world was a bitter, bitter experience. That bitterness is present on the Passover table in the form of horseradish or horseradish pickle. And a very good relish it is too: if you eat a heaped tablespoon of it, it sharpens your appetite. There is a poem by Ann Ridler which talks of 'the junk and treasure of an ancient creed'. All religious traditions include both, yours and mine. But what I have described here, and what we find in all religions, is treasure, not junk. I marvel at how Jews have turned their suffering and injustices into a menu of delight –

making bitterness an *hors d'oeuvre* and finding humour from persecution. Here is a story I heard one recent Passover, at the end of the evening when the celebrants have drunk four glasses of the wine of redemption.

From the Five Books of Moses we learn that only when the first person dared to plunge into the Red Sea did the waters actually part. How courageous that person must have been, say the commentators, but there is another folk explanation and it rings truer. When the Children of Israel got to the Red Sea, no one knew what to do. So someone pushed and said, 'You go first.' And another pushed and said, 'You go first,' and they all started pushing each other until someone fell into the Red Sea. And that is how the waters parted.

I hope you enjoy your bread of affliction. It's delicious with Cheddar cheese.

TWELVE

'It'

As a boy I was eager to learn but ignorant – and my parents, teachers and rabbis, who were usually so generous with advice and information, on this subject gave nothing away. I turned therefore to other sources. I read Leviticus, and learned all that I should not do (incest and women's clothes) but not what I should do, and how I should do it. The radio was more helpful. 'Birds do it,' sang the lady, and I listened intently. 'Bees do it – even educated fleas do it.' I turned this last piece of information over in my mind. It was a curious piece of the jigsaw, but as yet I could not determine its position or its relevance, so I listened to the lady once more. 'Let's do it,' she crooned, 'Let's do it again.' Again! Puberty was on the horizon, and

I was prepared to do it even if only once and die forever – if I ever learned how to, of course.

Did adults do it? The evidence pointed that way, but common sense revolted. If adults did it, then my parents must do it, which seemed unlikely, and my rabbi must do it, which seemed incredible. How could he do it? Would he wear his black gown or just his linen tabs, and surely he would have to keep his velvet hat on? Would he moan in English, Yiddish or Hebrew? This was exotic stuff. It was so absurd that I turned back to the birds, the bees, and the educated fleas.

I have been twenty years in the ministry, and religion has never lost this coyness. Four-letter words are respectable enough for the Oxford Dictionary but they can never make the pulpit, though my congregations, like everybody else, are doing it – and after doing it, do it again. This I know as a minister.

This coyness can be charming, but it is dangerous when religion and reality part company. Ordinary people have become more honest, and religious establishments have to catch up. Evasion is not purity, and the facts of life were not, after all, thought up by a dirty old man, but by divinity itself. I have, for example, seen three great changes in the last twenty years concerning 'it' which have scarcely been acknowledged in seminaries, even my own.

Sex has been separated from procreation and now wears no fig leaf of biological purpose. It has therefore to be considered as pleasure, and religion is not good with pleasure. Traditionally religion has used poverty and deprivation to provide the power for spiritual ascent. Yet sex and spirituality need each other. To accept the sexual needs of another person (emotional, physical and technical) requires a listening as profound as that required by prayer. Religious people preach and teach many lessons to the secular world. This is a lesson they have to learn from it.

A second change has affected the roles of the sexes. They are no longer fixed, and couples work out their own balance of functions and duties. This concerns washing up, cooking, sexual positions, and is beginning to affect ritual as well. A man can do the washing up, and a woman does not always have to look up at the ceiling. There is more muddle but there is also more experiment, more understanding, and more generosity.

A third change concerns the needs of sexual minorities which have scarcely been acknowledged, let alone understood. This has been a serious defect in the system, for their number is constant and their contribution to religion has been significant, if unacknowledged. Unfortunately they have been considered 'outsiders' – so those who need spirituality for their relationships (they have few social props) are precisely those who have been turned away from it.

I was heartened, though, by an article in the newspaper. One rabbi – the first in this country – had defied all precedent and come out with 'it', so to speak. If only this had happened in my childhood, all doubts would have been set at rest. Seven months pregnant in a maternity gown – a rabbi conducted a service. Truth was at last visible and I rejoiced.

I hasten to add, the rabbi was a woman.

THIRTEEN

Badly Used

When I was ordained I was so proud that I rushed to the synagogue and sat at my new desk in my new office waiting for my first clients. There was no great rush, but just as I was about to shut up shop a man knocked at the door. He was about to commit suicide, he said belligerently, and what was I f —— ing going to do about it!

I was startled and blurted out the first question in my mind. 'How are you going to do it?'

He stared at me in disbelief. 'What a question to ask!'

'Well, what am I supposed to ask?' I replied sulkily.

'You gotta tell me how wrong it is, see,' he said patiently.

'I can't very well,' I said, 'because when I tried it once, I bungled it.'

'I always do,' he said compassionately. We looked at each other and rocked with laughter. I made tea and we spent a cosy evening discussing all possible methods. We illustrated our arguments with gestures.

At two in the morning he said he would have to go, as he was on early shift that day – that's life! But he had enjoyed himself, and I had done him a power of good.

Not long after there was another tap at my door and I was visited by a North American lady in a hurry. I never knew her name but she reminded me of the tourist who rushed into the Louvre shouting, 'Where's the Mona Lisa, I'm double parked.'

I listened for an hour to her complex relations with her mother, several fathers, two lovers and a dawg. At the end I started to give her advice, but she shook her head. When she wanted advice she would go to her shrink, who, she said proudly, ground her into dust. She couldn't afford him at the moment, as she wanted to go shopping in Paris. I could only listen, she pointed out, and I wasn't up to much, but I was for free!

Though such interviews seemed funny at first, I began to get annoyed about how people used religion and me. When I got a job on the continent, the same

thing happened. But one day a Protestant minister asked to see me. Would I please unbaptise a hundred Jews and half Jews, he asked. He had handed out baptism certificates in Germany during the war, because this sometimes delayed their descent into the hell of the concentration camps.

'Were any of them really interested in Christianity?' I asked.

'Oh,' he said, 'how could I ask them, Rabbi Blue? It was wonderful for me at that time to be of use to anybody.'

From him I learned that allowing yourself to be used and even misused on occasion is what living and eternal living is about. (Don't overdo it – being a bathmat doesn't help you, or anybody who tramples over you.) Everyone knows it who deals with such tricky creatures as human beings like us, psychiatrists as well as ministers.

So here is a story of a psychiatrist who saw a Jewish woman and her neurotic son. After examining the lad, the psychiatrist said to the mother, 'Well, there's nothing wrong with your Issy, except for a slightly overdeveloped Oedipus complex.'

'Ach, doctor,' she said, 'Oedipus, Shmoedipus, vot do I care, so long as he loves his mummy.'

FOURTEEN

Peace Inside and Out

In the forties and fifties, when I was in my teens and early twenties, I longed for revolution, and at that time my desire was appeased for a lot of them took place. As soon as I turned on the wireless, I got another helping of insurrection, as the announcer informed me that another bastion of privilege had fallen. I do not want to make a joke of it because there was a lot of entrenched nastiness about. There was an awful lot of entrenched nastiness in me too, which I didn't care to examine. I couldn't help noticing that my own motives were not pure and shining zeal for the welfare of others. Part of me – the intellectual part – excused the necessary mayhem, but part of me – the instinctive part – enjoyed it. In fact I was titillated by the blood and guts. Among the socio-economic theories I espoused some little crawly things were hidden – my aggressions, my bitterness, and the remnants of sado-masochist erotica from early puberty. It took me much longer to be as honest about myself as I was about society. Indeed I have never succeeded. To be frank about others is no great hardship. It is seductively easy and enjoyable.

The revolutions I noted down so eagerly succeeded each other too quickly to be convincing. One lot of reformers had scarcely got in when they were replaced by their more revolutionary successors. Unfortunately the more closely I looked, I couldn't help remarking how little had changed. Recently I met someone who had had analysis. He had been taken apart, he told me triumphantly, and had been put together again. 'Mm,' said a mutual friend, 'and it's been so well done you can't tell the difference.'

Well, that's the way it has been with so many of my revolutions. So much has happened, yet there has been little change. That's the way, I think, it must always be, until a revolution also takes place within the revolutionary. A colleague of mine once said to me, 'No matter how you cut the salami, it's still the same salami.' Most revolutions cut the salami in different slices, but what they deal out is the same – adjustments to consumerism and comfort, and re-direction of aggression, not its elimination. This explains why revolutions go wrong. The ideals are fine, but they can never flower, because they are hijacked by the ego.

I notice my own aggression when I am standing impatiently in a queue, or pleading with a bureaucrat, or irritated with those who cross me. Most people are astonished by the strength of their negative feelings – I am no exception.

I don't think you can bring peace to the world outside unless you have achieved some peace within. The former cannot wait for the latter, but it is essential that both activities go along at the same time. It is easy to think you are dealing with the cosmos, when you are only projecting on to it your childhood hang-ups – a humiliating but necessary thought.

FIFTEEN

Martin and Marx

I sat in a café in East Berlin enjoying the old-world atmosphere of that city of the future. East Berlin is shabby, but comfortable and cosy, like the London East End of my childhood or Liverpool without the Beatle bounce. It's a Puritan city and I think many religionists of the conservative sort would like it if they were not so prejudiced, for it is ordered, certain and polite. We are in the best of all possible worlds, the slogans assure us, on the big red banners which festoon the modern glass buildings and on the little banner which drapes the greying merchandise in the little corset shop opposite to where I sit. I had expected East Berlin to be nasty in the James Bond manner; in fact I found it rather restful. Well, you live and learn. Who would have thought before Luther's 500th birthday celebrations there, when so many similarities were discovered by the authorities between Marx and Martin, that they had so much in common. The only bond between them I had ever heard of was a common distaste for Jews.

The west, too, has its certainties. A spiritual leader has advertised in a daily newspaper his formula for Utopia and we have been notified that TV evangelists, American-style, may soon pop up in our pubs and parlours via cable television, with their promise of speedy salvation and their short cuts to happiness. Well, the sophisticated may criticise, but they genuinely interest me. For like many jokers I find the world a sad place and relief is welcome, whatever the source.

I come from a family of believers and as a child I longed to share their faiths. I say faiths because they had as many beliefs as there are systems in bridge, and they proclaimed them with equal fervour. They all wanted a trip to heaven, but some just got taken for a ride. During their passionate arguments around the dinner table, I used to look up as a child and saw my mother give the assembled theists and materialists a good-natured smile and me a tolerant, unbelieving wink. I heard this joke in East Berlin, and its irreverence reminded me of my mother's wink.

After one of the astronauts came down and paraded in Red Square, Khrushchev asked to see him privately. 'Ah, comrade,' he said, 'I want to ask you a very delicate question!'

The astronaut nodded dolefully.

'When you were up there in outer space did you see Him? Does God exist?'

'I did and He does,' replied the astronaut.

'Mmmmm,' said Khrushchev, 'I always thought so, but for the sake of our state and our party, promise me you'll never mention it to anyone.'

The astronaut promised.

The astronaut went on a tour of the world and in the west he met an important religious leader. When they were alone the religious leader whispered urgently, 'When you were up there in outer space, did you see Him? Does God exist?'

'I didn't and He doesn't,' replied the loyal astronaut.

'Mmmmm,' said the religious leader, 'I always thought so, but for the sake of good relations between our systems never mention it, please, to anyone.'

The bewildered astronaut promised a second time.

SIXTEEN

A Tall Story from the Talmud

In the recesses of the Talmud, the collected rabbinical writings of nearly two thousand years ago, there is buried a strange story. It says a lot – I think – though I don't quite know what and I don't know on what level to take it, or whether it is serious or comic or both – probably the last. Anyway here it is, and see what you make of it.

It concerns a type of oven; Rabbi Eleazer said it was ritually clean but the other rabbis said it wasn't. Rabbi Eleazer said: 'If I'm right in my interpretation of the scripture let this tree prove it,' and lo and behold the tree was blown a hundred ells away. (No, I don't know what an ell is. I get muddled enough by the metric system.)

Then he said, 'If I'm right, let the walls of this academy verify it,' and lo and behold the walls started to lean over.

But his opponent Rabbi Joshua argued with the walls. He said to them, 'Rabbinical arguments are no business of yours!'

Well, the walls didn't fall down, because they had too much regard for Rabbi Joshua, and they didn't straighten up, out of respect for Rabbi Eleazer. And, says the Talmud, that's how they remain to this day. You can take it or leave it.

Then heaven got into the act, and a voice said, 'Rabbi Eleazer is right.'

But Rabbi Joshua retorted: 'The place for deciding legal disputes isn't in heaven.'

What did he mean by that? He meant that the five books of Moses say quite clearly that they are decided by an authoritative body on earth, not by heaven.

Now I think Rabbi Joshua was right. The answer to a lot of problems is not in signs or wonders. They are not the answers to our problems and I wouldn't advise looking for them. But in another way he was wrong, because the kingdom of heaven is already inside us and among us. When you pray, hold up your ordinary life to the light of God, and you will find something very extraordinary on it – His fingerprints. Among the confusion of voices in your mind is His still small voice. It's more reliable than a miracle. If, of course, you do have a vision or hear a voice, then you are still left with a problem, as in this instance.

A Jew fell over a precipice. As he fell he clutched the branch of a little tree which was growing from the side of the cliff. In his despair, as he hung there, he started to pray, 'If there is anybody up there, come and help me.'

Well, a voice did come from heaven, and it boomed out, 'Don't worry, I shall answer thy plea. Just let go, and the palm of My hand will support thee and bring thee up.'

There was a long pause. Then the Jew prayed again and asked, 'Is there anybody else up there?'

SEVENTEEN

A Helping Hand

Shortly after I was ordained, I was appointed religious director for Europe, because there was no one else. All my competition had gone up in smoke, literally. I was the bishop of a bankrupt diocese whose congregants were mainly ghosts, and I was told to get on with it.

I wandered in a bewildered way from country to country. I had little money, copious only in blessing. So I went round blessing everyone in sight. I prayed in Dutch for Queen Juliana and *'het hele koninglijke huis'*. I asked God to rain down blessings, in both Flemish and French, on King Baudouin and Queen Fabiola. I was also careful not to slight by omission the Grand Duchess of Luxembourg. Presidents, of course, were not so classy, but I practised my accent for the Presidents of France of both the 4th and 5th Republics and doled out a kind, though distant, prayer for German Chancellors both East and West. It was good clean fun in a difficult time. Egged on by the liturgy, I got addicted to blessings. I asked God in a variety of languages to keep an eye on the bereaved and the suffering, the military and the mothers, agricultural workers and people in the media, domestic pets, social workers and women.

I could have gone on forever, because there is no logical point at which to stop. The sentiments flow so smoothly, and helping third parties is easy if it doesn't cost you anything. You seem so benevolent, even to yourself, that you get uppity and imagine your love is God's love or an exceedingly close relation to it. At times I wondered at my own benevolence.

But I also began to wonder what on earth I was up to. Did these blessings of mine change anything? It certainly didn't look like it. The world is a tough nut, and it doesn't etherealise as easily as prayers suggest. Spirit is all very well, but for practical purposes, as any DIY person can tell you, you need hands. But God is an invisible spirit, who has no hands, and I panicked. Was I just dishing out opium for the masses and food for my own gluttonous ego? This was a most unwelcome thought, as I enjoyed religion and liked being a rabbi, and didn't want to become a solicitor.

I decided I would have to step in and make up the deficiency myself if I wanted to carry on with my own self-respect. I would have to be God's hands. I am an egocentric person, and only reluctantly came to the conclusion that if I wanted to go on speaking about blessings, I would have to try to *be* a blessing. I have not been very successful, but I have at least managed to remain in the rabbinate.

Here is a tip from a religious professional. Be careful about blessings. Your prayers may not change the world, but they may change you, and this is not really what you intended. I can pray sincerely, 'Blessed are You, Lord, who answers prayer' – though I would have preferred an answer which didn't hit back.

EIGHTEEN

Hitch-hiking to Atonement

Recently I was with a group of Jewish refugees who were discussing times gone by, a favourite Jewish occupation. One remembered her palace in Alexandria, another his vineyard in the Carpathians, another her house in Unter den Linden in Berlin. The bitterness for their lost homes had long gone: they had learnt the great art of giving up.

It is difficult giving up good things but it is even more difficult giving up bad things. We go through life tied to a cartload of rubbish, to injustices and

enmities of long ago, to humiliations and defeats that should have been forgotten. And it is even more difficult for nations than for individuals. In fact it seems wrong to want to give up – we feel traitors. So we carry around some frightening luggage of un-purified hatred, filled with bombs.

I myself tried to go to Germany three or four times after the war, but each time I stopped before the frontier. I was hampered by my own hostility, crippled by my distrust. And even when I got across on business, I knew the frontier still remained in me.

Crude economics did what refined theology couldn't. No one really believed in the small Jewish survivor communities I served, so I had a long ecclesi-astical title but little money to back it up. I felt like a bishop of a bankrupt diocese. Then I remembered my student days, ditched the title and began to hitch my way around the Fatherland.

At last I met people, and Germany took on a human face. I met gypsies on the road, whose families had been shot at sight without the 'luxury' of a concen-tration camp. In Hamburg cafés I met homosexuals, whose friends had been beheaded. People didn't think enough about the Jews in the thirties, and we,

I suppose, never thought enough about our fellow-sufferers either. It helped me to realise that we had no monopoly of suffering.

I met soldiers and ex-party members too. I was stuck in a railway coach one night in a snowdrift, with a brass band going to a competition. I provided some schnapps, they provided the music, and as the music died down and the schnapps was finished we really met, and did not just *talk* about meeting.

I wandered into a nationalist rally in a backwoods German village. They had never met a rabbi before and listened with a sense of shock as I expressed my feelings in startlingly bad Yiddish. They sent me Christmas cards for many years.

A girl asked me to forgive her. As we talked, I realised that she had lost her parents, her home, the lot, in the war, and I from the security of Britain had lost little. But which of us had the right to forgive, or to wear the mantle of Anne Frank?

In Germany I had great power, much more than in my own country. I stood on a pulpit and people turned towards it, not because of me or the small survivor community I represented, but because its foundations were six million Jewish dead. But what sermon does one give from such a terrible eminence? It is not hard to create guilt, to shift burdens on to innocent shoulders, to rivet sin on to people with iron, and leave them with no way out. We do such things, after all, every day of our lives to each other. It was more difficult to locate the Nazi in me, and the Jew in them, and find a way for us all to find release. In scripture the dead may bury the dead. In life it is the living who have to do it.

Every religion has its rituals of forgiveness for individuals. There is the Day of Atonement, there is Lent, there is confession. But nations and groups need to be purified, too, and there is no ritual for them. And if you speak of such things to political students, they say you are naïve and silly. So a lot of guilt remains in the air, and it goes sour and turns into bitterness and hatred, and each one of us is left to find his own way home spiritually – to hitch-hike to atonement.

NINETEEN

In the Best Taste

I'm a peasant – I know it. I do hear the harmonies of the spirit, but they send me to sleep. I was at the opera: her breast heaved as she moaned 'Tristan'; his breast heaved as he cried 'Isolde': I was heaved out of my seat because I was asleep and snoring.

I don't often see genuine visions either, though I try. I wiggle my eyelids, but it's a toss-up whether I focus on the beatific vision or on a Coca-Cola bottle – my left eye is astigmatic. So I have to get to the highest truths through the lowest of the senses. It is my taste buds which lead me to love, both human and divine, which guide me through the tragedies of life, and on which I rely for a foretaste of heaven.

With human love the connection came early. I was shy and clumsy and could only squeeze her hand. She was virtuous but very practical. Would I get her, she asked, some kosher kiss-proof vegetarian lipstick? When she licked her lips, what was she licking? she asked herself. It was better not to think of it! She gracefully indicated that one day I might lick her lips too, and she really couldn't take the religious responsibility. Well, I dashed across the Channel and returned triumphant. She was grateful, and my first taste of love was comforting, clean and kosher. Since then standards of taste have declined – everyone says so – and, alas, I am no exception.

I never learned divine love in a seminary but in my grandmother's kitchen. She gave me spoonfuls of

horseradish to remember the slavery of Egypt and the bitterness of exile. As I grew to like the taste, my theology never got sorted out. We celebrated the triumph of Esther with poppy-seed cakes, and the triumph of the Maccabees with nuts. I liked the Revelation of the Law because Mount Sinai was always sour cream and sugar on a plateau of cheesecake. On the other hand I never took to the Jewish New Year because that meant apples and honey. I bit through a worm with my first apple, so that lovely festival still retains an oddly tragic taste for me.

As you can see, my theology is easily rocked. It changes whenever I go to a dentist. Saliva floods my mouth and gall floods into my soul. The pump works overtime as if it were trying to bale out Britain with North Sea oil. Then one day the assistant at the dentist asked me how I would like my fluoride. Would I like bitter lemon flavour, she enquired patiently, or, sizing me up, wild cherry or raspberry? Had she got chocolate or banana, I asked? No, she said, the children didn't want those. In wonder I chose wild cherry. When I naïvely expressed my delight, my dentist asked me where I had lived, and said casually that the jungle began in Watford. Be that as it may, in cherry blossom time I no longer think of temples in Japan but of fluoride on my gums, and the sheer good taste of National Health.

At the crematorium, too, where I officiate, death has lost something of its sting. The café there is so nice, like the teashops of my childhood – the tea is hot, and the tea ladies so helpful. If you'll pardon the expression, it's the crème de la crem.

And what about the foretaste of heaven? According to tradition we'll eat leviathan, which will be nice as I like fish, though I'm curious about the sauce. I am not so happy about nectar and ambrosia. They sound too sweet, and I don't enjoy Sauternes.

If you think this is too frivolous, then take down your Bible and turn to Psalm 34, verse 8 – 'O taste and see that the Lord is good.' You see, God doesn't leave out peasants like me!

TWENTY

A Blessing over Underwear

I was invited to take part in an ecumenical service. Would I please, the invitation said, wear full canonicals, as we were all going to march in procession. I replied with alacrity, because I had just seen *Aïda* at Covent Garden, and nobody there had offered me a walk-on part, though every bit of me wanted to join in. In my childhood I had marched against capitalism and fascism, and even occasionally against socialism, because I was an amiable child who just didn't like to say no. I also needed some congenial exercise, being no good at ball games. When I was evacuated during the war I had also marched against the demon drink to please my foster parents, until I was cuffed by my grandfather, who held very different views.

So there I was in billowing black robes festooned with odd bits of silver, looking like a Jewish Christmas tree. In front of me were monks and nuns carrying a cross, and civic dignitaries, and behind me a pavane of clergy in a froth of surplices, and a high ecclesiastic who outdid the flowers of the field as well as Solomon in all his glory.

It was a tremendous service. Trumpets brayed from the gallery, and the organ and choirs were worthy of Ronnie Scott's. Finally, after a lot of ecclesiastical choreography, a young lady danced her faith before us. I didn't know where to look as the only precedent I could recall was Salome, whose motives were not the same. If I looked at her with interest, it seemed unspiritual. But if I avoided her eyes, it made me look shifty. So I did what many of the other clergymen did – I looked benignly eighteen inches to the right or left of her, which might appear as good piety or bad contact lenses.

While I was eye-dodging through professional cowardice, I realised how imprisoned I was by words. You can bless God in many ways, not only with words or with your mind, but also with your body. You can bless Him with a generous deed or in music or even by the way you dress.

I remembered the Jewish blessings I had been taught to say as a child when I put on my clothes. When I put on my belt, I used to say, 'Blessed art Thou, O Lord our God, who girdest Israel with strength.' When I put on my shoes I used to say, 'Blessed art Thou, O Lord our God, who makest firm the steps of man.' When I was aware of the differences between little boys and little girls and their clothing, I used to say, 'Blessed art Thou, O Lord our God, who hast not made me a woman.' (I hasten to add that because of Women's Lib I no longer use this blessing.) There was a blessing for every stitch I wore. Sometimes I get jaded by words, especially religious words, because I use too many, too casually, and they become useless for prayer. Once or twice I tried to dance a blessing but I am too middle-aged, and the result might be pleasing in the eyes of God but in

nobody else's, not even my own. So sometimes I put on the fringed robe (the same kind that Jesus wore) and bless the Lord as I put on my shoes and belt and vest and pants with piety. Heaven can attach itself to your underwear as well as to your reason.

TWENTY-ONE

A Happy New Year!

If you live in a middle-class Jewish suburb, and it is late summer, you might be woken up before breakfast by a braying sound from your neighbour's garden. It is so shrill and so insistent, you might think it is the end of the world.

Well, for your Jewish neighbour it is – sort of. He has been practising on the ram's horn – 'an ill wind that no one blows good', in the words of the comedian

Danny Kaye. No one blows it good because the horn is so ancient – it has no modern innards, no reed or whistle. I myself have never been able to coax a note out of it. But then I can't whistle either.

Although the liturgy for the Jewish New Year says, 'Happy the people, who hear this joyous sound', it sounds really more like an air raid alarm or an early warning system. Judgment, it says, is coming to everyone. All that you tried to hide in the last year from your neighbours, from your nearest and dearest, and especially from yourself is coming under review. You have a last chance to put everything right in the ten days after the New Year. Then comes the great Day of Atonement and the foretaste of your own last judgment.

Now this is not a cosy thought, and though there are a lot of sweet things to eat on the Jewish New Year, you can't help eating them rather thoughtfully. The pots of honey which Jewish people consume with slices of apple, or cooked with carrots and brisket, or mixed in honey cake cannot sweeten the terrible dilemmas of Jewish life.

Israel never loses a war, but can it ever win a real peace? The Palestinians in their camps look so much like Jews – but they are not Jews, are they? They are Palestinians. What happens if the political struggles of the Middle East join themselves to religious struggles and both together make a cocktail – one of those explosive cocktails you find in Northern Ireland – which make men drunk or mad? Will we Jews ever find a way to a Jewish life in a Marxist state or will the bitterness between us endure forever? Will the terrible cycle of western life be repeated in our time – boom, slump and unemployment, pass the buck and Auschwitz? Why shouldn't it happen again? People haven't changed in the last forty years, have they?

But even these questions don't go deep enough, because they are about other people, living in other places at other times, and the New Year is not just about them, it is about me now. Not the masks life has taught me to wear, but the naked me stripped of my 'wardrobe of excuses'. It is terrifying to see yourself as you really are, and know yourself as the murderer and the victim, the oppressor and the oppressed, the manipulator who manipulates himself.

And all this goes through my mind on the Jewish New Year which celebrates the birthday of the world, as I meet my friends in their best clothes, and we eat honey cake together. That's the flavour of Jewish life and Jewish festivals, bitter-sweet, holding together happiness and insecurity, pride and shame, triumph and tragedy.

My grandfather – may he rest in peace – on the New Year used to wish everyone Gentile luck – because Jewish luck, he said, isn't up to much. So, like him, I wish you Gentile luck and a Happy New Year, Jewish-style.

TWENTY-TWO

Dust and Ashes

Here is a story about the Jewish Day of Atonement, the most solemn and serious fast in the Jewish Year. As the service was about to begin, a hush came over the assembled congregation. The venerable rabbi held out his hand for silence. Instead of going to his pulpit, he approached the Holy Ark with tears in his eyes. He flung open the doors and prostrated himself before the scrolls with their white mantles, the symbols of purity and repentance.

'Lord,' he said in a strained voice, 'have mercy on me, for I am only dust and ashes.'

After his confession the congregation watched him as he arose and took his place at the reading desk. He opened his prayer book, and was about to commence the solemn service.

But before he could do so, the cantor of the synagogue said gently, 'Wait!' He too approached the Holy Ark, and following his venerable rabbi in all things, gently opened the doors of the Ark, and prostrated himself humbly before the scrolls.

'Lord,' he said, 'I too seek mercy, for I too am just dust and ashes.'

In the silence, he took his place at the reading desk, and signed to the rabbi that the service could begin.

But there was yet one more confession to be heard, from the humblest servant of the synagogue. The beadle moved forward from the door with tears in his eyes. And while the congregation watched, moved and astonished, he too climbed the steps to the Ark with bowed head. He opened its door lovingly, and also prostrated himself, and spoke piously and gently.

'Lord,' he said, 'have mercy on me, a sinner, who is but dust and ashes.'

The rabbi breathed deeply and turned to the cantor. 'Look,' he said, 'who presumes to think he is only dust and ashes!'

I don't know how this story takes you, but it certainly pricked me, and as I laughed I could feel all my pomposity and ecclesiasticism oozing out of me. The humour deflated me as effectively as hours of agonising on my knees. The funny thing is that when I try to remember my sins, all I end up with is my foibles. It takes a joke to hit me below the belt, and take the stuffing out of me.

It's very easy in religion to miss the point, to get so interested in the symbols and signs that you forget what they are supposed to symbolise or what the signs are supposed to point to. Tapping your chest or your bosom during a confession can be fun, very unlike the stab of piercing pain that comes with real loss.

In the scriptures, yours and mine, God is jealous or wrath or loving, but He hardly ever laughs, and doesn't wink. Nor is there any official blessing for jokes, even those which purge you. So I will have to make one up: 'Blessed are You, Lord our God, King of the Universe, Whose love is manifest in laughter.'

TWENTY-THREE

Plastic Piety

When I was in America, I was given a little matchbox. It had a knob on the front marked 'Resurrection', and when you pressed it the box sprang open and a little plastic man, previously prone, now sat up, surprised but smiling. I was much taken with it, and put it away carefully with a clockwork rabbi who swayed when you wound him up, and a phosphorescent saint who glowed green in the dark.

I have always had an extravagant taste in objects of piety, and became very fond of a pulpit which rose electronically in the air, leaving me like a monkey on a stick. I was also fascinated by a Temple where the lights turned blue and played on my features as I said memorial prayers. A Christian friend told me of a shrine with a slot machine: when you put a coin in, the saint ascended through showers of flowers. I don't think I could become a devotee, but I could become an addict. No, I am not bothered about pious vulgarity. After all, God is supposed to be more at home in Jerusalem than in Bond Street, and a lapse of taste is a mistake, not a sin.

I do not underrate such toys because, like all the great rites and ceremonies, and indeed religion itself, they are devices which help us to glimpse the invisible, and to make eternity domestic and livable. But I am careful not to overrate them either. I have become

fond of my pulpit, and my worn, frayed gown, and I am grateful to my traditions because through them I have met God. But I must remember I do not worship my traditions. I worship the reality they point to. I worship God, not the means to Him.

Some of the most terrible religious wars and persecutions have taken place because loyal worshippers transferred the loyalty that only God can command to the devices we use to keep our minds fixed on Him. It is a simple and well-intentioned error, but in human history it is an error which has caused great suffering and even murder. In religion you need a good head as well as a good heart, and also a sense of humour.

My most effective religious memory device is the Mezuzah. This is a small metal or wooden case fixed to the doorpost in the doorways of Jewish homes. In it is a little piece of parchment reminding all who enter of God's presence, and of our duty to love Him. Pious Jews kiss it as they enter. It recalls us all to holiness, and few Jewish houses are without one. Here is a story about a Mezuzah I heard from a pious colleague.

A Jewish family moved into a street, and their non-Jewish neighbours were very intrigued when they saw them nail a Mezuzah on to their door.

'What is it?' they asked.

'Oh, it's only a little case with some verses of the Bible written on parchment, rolled up in it. It is called a Mezuzah.'

'Thank you,' they said, 'for the explanation.' But they didn't believe it – 'You know what Jews are,' they said – and one night, when the Jewish family were out, they stole over and hurriedly detached the Mezuzah.

Sure enough, inside it was a little strip of parchment, as they had been told. Feverishly they unrolled it, and written in it they read: 'Help, I am a prisoner in a Mezuzah factory!'

TWENTY-FOUR

Damn!

I started to peer at her over the edge of my pulpit –
though one shouldn't peep – because she looked
so jolly uncomfortable. And as I took the service I
occasionally looked up from my prayer book and stole
a glance at her, because I was curious as to what
would happen to her.

She was obviously not used to synagogues or to
services, and this was her once-a-year social call on
her Creator. I wondered why she had come at all.
Perhaps to say memorial prayers for the religion of
her grandparents that died? Ancestor worship is always the last faith to crumble. Her dress was subdued
but expensive. It was also very new, and she creaked!
After two or three blessings there was a discreet
wiggle and an adjustment of buckles and straps.
She conscientiously tried to follow the square black
Hebrew letters, but occasionally she looked up from
her devotions in a puzzled way at the eternal light.
What was she asking? Probably the same questions
asked by saint or sinner alike: 'Is there anybody there?
If so, what's in it for me?'

As she was not at her ease, little things started to
go wrong. She dropped a hanky and nearly lost a
shoe. The handbag was saved by a quick leap which
distracted me and made me lose my place, so the
choir sang the wrong Amen. But she was not going
to give up. In a high, precise voice, she implored God,
polite but surprised, 'to quicken the dead', 'to rebuild
the walls of Jerusalem' and 'to keep His faith with
those who sleep in the dust'. Instinctively she removed a speck of it with a shaped fingernail.

How long, how long O Lord, I wondered, could
she continue in this unnatural state, wearing clothes
unadapted to her body, saying things irrelevant to

her interests and being anybody but herself?

The silent prayers made her feel worse – as they often do. A brooch came adrift. Then a glove. Then it was all too much. She slouched back defeated. Then I saw her lips move, and I knew she said 'Damn!' She had tried to do the right thing, but the more right it was supposed to be, the more wrong it felt.

I felt so happy for her then. For the first time she was herself, not a mask or a projection, or a nice person sucking up to the Almighty, or a conforming child, who knew which side her cosmic bread was buttered. And because she was herself, prayer was possible. In fact it had already taken place and been answered, though she didn't know it. Something inside her had wanted freedom, and lo and behold, her shell had cracked. Is not that a wonder?

Whether it brought her pleasure or pain I don't know – religion brings both – but she had become real. We often confuse our ragbag of desires, our mental fluff, with the real prayer of our being, and we wonder why God hasn't paid more attention to our rubbish. Fortunately He is selective in what He listens to. 'Blessed are you Lord, who listens to prayer' – if the prayer is worth listening to, that is.

TWENTY-FIVE

A Nice Little Religion

I now want to tell you something about the dying, the afflicted and the handicapped. I am not going to tell you how I coped with them or what I gave them, for it is not worth a mention. This is the truth, not humility. I shall tell you instead what they gave me, which was both definite and considerable.

When I was becoming a minister, I tried as sincerely as I could to be false. It came out of an early childhood confusion: I thought that pleasing people was goodness. So I acquired a grey flannel suit, and shiny shoes, a warm handshake, and a shiny smile that was friendly but not familiar. My community thought I was a doll, and we 'shlapped nuchus' from each other, which meant in Yiddish that we buttered each other up nicely. I served them up the opium of the masses in measured doses, and they tranquillised me with respect and compliments. We huddled together against the cold of the cosmos under the blanket of tradition. Like most middle-class people we wanted God for security. The religious life was clean thoughts in clean underwear, and the aim of our prayers was to tidy up the cosmos and make it nice.

But it wasn't really nice, and indeed never could be. This became clear when I was called out to dying people. I tried to say nice things, ecclesiastical things, to them, and they just looked at me with compassion and irony. My pretensions were pricked by their weary politeness, their courage and their occasional humour. I was forced to examine again my little box of spiritual goodies and my theological sleight of hand. I felt like a pedlar of dud watches or cheap disposable toys. My compassion was professional, and my feeling fear. The cosmos was greater, grander and more awesome than I had ever allowed myself to believe.

It contained more love and more indifference than was good for my sanity. There was more sadness in it, more life and more courage than my nice little religion could cope with.

And so it died, that little religion of mine, like the bodies of those I visited. One day in hospital I ventured to speak of it to them, and for the first time a flash of recognition passed between us. We looked at each other and knew we were in the same boat, carried along by the same stream, guided by the same principle. Against our will we were forced to grow up. I had to grow into the life of an adult as they had to grow into the life of eternity. Neither of us wanted it, but life is not there to serve us – we are there to serve it.

Being with dying people was very important for me. I learned that, without death, life has no frame to give it shape, no reference to give it proportion. When you can face death, truth breaks in. Truth doesn't make you cosy, but it does make you free. 'O God full of compassion, whose presence is over us, grant perfect rest beneath the shelter of your presence with the holy and pure, who shine as the lights of the firmament, to the dying people who gave me a living faith. May we come together in the gathering of life.'

TWENTY-SIX

The By-products of Affliction

When I meet afflicted people I meet my own inadequacy. The gap between what I am and what I ought to be is clear and painful. I try to do the right thing. I think about them, and how I can help them or be of service. I feel I ought to cheer them up, though with what I do not know, for I have no great resources of cheer within me. So sometimes I become hearty instead, and apply more ointment to my ego than thought to their problems. I can't tell you, therefore, how I have helped them, because I haven't. I can only tell you of how they have helped me. It is right to think about such things, for who knows when affliction no longer means them or us but me?

From afflicted people I learned a very valuable lesson, about which there is a conspiracy of silence. Many problems just have no answer, so it's no use trying to invent one. You can only learn to live with the problems or transcend them. It's no use saying they will go away and that there is a happy ending in this world for everyone – for this is not true – though you can try for it. If you are visiting an afflicted person, over-hopeful chatter gets you off the hook, if your visit isn't too long, but you can tell by the expression on people's faces that they know you're playing the game to help yourself, not to help them.

It's also no use pretending that God isn't in it or involved. If He isn't, then He is only present in buttercups, and simply divine with daisies, and who wants that sort of twaddle – not a person in pain. And it's no good saying that suffering sanctifies you and pain redeems you. Sometimes it does, sometimes it doesn't. You need some energy even for sanctification, and suffering or intense pain strips you, so that you don't have much energy left. You need every bit you've got just to hold on.

But there is something more. I have met some afflicted people who were not especially saintly or particularly pious. They certainly did not ask God to forgive them. Many felt it was *their* job to forgive *Him*. But they knew that the centre of the world was not in the world, and in their affliction and in their pain they managed to fix their attention on God and keep it there. This was an important lesson for me. Even when you are religious, even when you are religious professionally, and your job depends on it, you doubt.

You can suppress that doubt, but it is like an affliction – you have to live with it. And when you meet an afflicted person who believes, even in his hour of pain, it helps you to believe even in your moment of doubt.

In the afflictions and suffering of the Nazi period some Jews hid in cellars. On a cellar wall an afflicted person whose name I shall never know had scrawled these words:

I believe in the Sun – even when I do not see it
I believe in love – even when I do not feel it
I believe in God – even when He is not present

On such affliction my faith is built.

TWENTY-SEVEN

Catch-22

I am a healthy person, who has relied on handicapped people all my life. There are people I know who from time to time have to opt out of life. The black clouds of depression gather on the horizon of their minds. Soon they blot out the light and the hope in their lives. Everything will become unsure, infirm and ambiguous – the curtains of their room, their God, the walls and themselves. They will have to hang on until those strange clouds return to where they came, and withdraw. Then they will be able to stretch out a shaky hand, and touch the curtains, and dare to peer into the street.

I go to such people for hope and for comfort, whenever life gets too much for me, or I am tripped up by my ambition or my greed. They are teachers who have taught me to hang on. Their diplomas are genuine, from the school of suffering, and I am the benficiary: 'Blessed are You, Lord, King of the Universe,

who has shared His wisdom with those who fear Him.'

My liveliest friend is confined to a wheelchair. She can sometimes do little more than wiggle her hand or turn her head. Each illness she has had has worked against the other, and her life has been for years and years a Catch-22 situation, 'trapped like a trap in a trap'.

I visit her for happiness and to enjoy myself. We moan, we complain and we laugh. We ask questions, the real questions, and don't worry when we don't get the answers. She is alive and fights for life – the life of a human being, not a cabbage. I first went to see her to comfort her. Now I am worried she might find me a bore (ministers' visits often are) and turn to livelier things. 'Blessed are You, Lord, the life of existence.'

A girl had a metal arm. They offered her a piece of flesh-coloured plastic to cover it. It looked very real and very dead. But she had the luck to meet someone who kissed her, and removed the plastic. He exclaimed how beautiful, and shiny, and chic was her metal claw. Love gives you courage – she ventured to look at her artificial arm intently. She considered it, and then thought she would set a glowing ruby in the dull metal. It should be very beautiful. 'Blessed are You, Lord, who varies the forms of His creatures.'

This is a story from an old Jewish tradition. There was once a king who had a beautiful diamond, and he was very proud of it because it was unique. But one day the diamond got deeply scratched and nobody could remove the scratch or repair the fault, and the king was very sad. Then a jeweller came who said he could make the diamond even better than it was before. The king doubted him at first, but then entrusted him with the stone. And when the workman had finished, the king saw that he had engraved around the flaw a lovely rosebud, and the ugly scratch had become the stem.

TWENTY-EIGHT
A Blithe Spirit

The Spirit came to me many years ago at Oxford. It was there I first tasted its fruits. I was walking down St Giles when I saw a notice that there would be a Meeting of Friends – the Quakers – on Thursday afternoon. It was Thursday, so I decided to go and view them, because I was curious about Gentiles and what they got up to in their churches and meetings. The pious from the University weren't there, thank

God, only cheery Quaker farmers from the country-side around.

We sat in a cosy room. Someone said a cosy prayer, and we waited. I stared at a vase of flowers, and tried to think of God or whatever, but I could only think of Van Gogh and his wretched sunflowers. I hadn't prayed for years, but decided to have another dab at it. I was composing prayers quite nicely, when I got tripped by that dreadful lispy repro English and re-lapsed into a sulky silence. There didn't seem much in it for me. What set it off I don't know, but a Spirit uncoiled in the silence, and by it I touched eternal life. I testified, but I don't remember what I said. I decided never to testify again. I was too garrulous and my Spirit was blithe but vulgar.

I thought about it afterwards and told myself that things like that don't happen to people like me. In fact I was quite shocked, for I was a conventional materialist and an ideological Marxist who relied on his intellect not his intuition. I had betrayed the truth and reality – whatever they are – and had whored after mystery. I calmed down and decided it was an interesting sideshow but it wasn't life. Nevertheless I decided to carry on with it, because it might give me more understanding of the Middle Ages, and as I was a history student that wouldn't be bad.

But I had invoked more than I realised. The Spirit pulled me like a magnet, and after it I tumbled into Quaker meetings, Christian crypts and Jewish syna-gogues, keeping blind dates with God-knows-what. It wasn't its power which got me, but its gentleness. I don't go for macho stuff – even on a cosmic scale. Strange changes started taking place inside me, like rumblings in the tummy, or in crucibles in a labora-tory. Intuitions were bubbling away, and strange qual-ities were crystallising in my mind and my heart.

I gave up my seat for an old lady in a train, and God-knows-what within me nodded. Someone admired my tie. It was pink roses on blue satin and I was proud of it. With only a second's hesitation – because I was still of this world, you know – I took it off and pressed it into his hands. An extravagant gesture, but with the Spirit where do you stop?

The Spirit certainly didn't make me tranquil, as St Paul promises, for a few months after I ended up on a psychoanalyst's couch. Nor did I ever convert anyone properly to God – except perhaps myself. But there were some unexpected results. I sat in a synagogue and prayed, 'Lord, if You can't make me a saint, why not try to make me a gentleman.' And that prayer has been successful on occasion.

TWENTY-NINE

Life on the Brink

In the café I brooded about my pay, prospects and job security – though I was only in my twenties – when the two of them burst in. He was debonair in a floppy hat, and she glittered in a diamanté cloak. He fondled her, as she fondled a red rose. They had met in Paris. They had fallen deliriously in love, and they were well into their eighties. He commanded champagne, and we toasted 'Life on the brink'.

Now brinkmanship is the story of my life. I've been wondering, for example, whether I could tell you the wonderful story about the two Jewish women who went on a safari holiday to Africa, and in the bush they were attacked by a gorilla who . . . but I'm sorry, it's too near the brink, and you'll have to wait for the ending. Sometimes I've gone over the brink – when I fell into a grave while I was taking a funeral on an icy winter morning.

But it's clear: all of us have to get adjusted to living on a nuclear brink. Even if America or Russia don't drop the bomb, or mislay it, some third-world psychopath will find it irresistible, for bangs boost the ego. It's no use running to religion for rescue, for life doesn't work that way, no matter how many prayers you mumble. But prayer can give you the courage to live on the brink with it. For prayer doesn't wish the world away or make its problems disappear; it gives us the courage to live with them as they are, in the world as it is. In prayer we are reminded that the world dies to us every night as we fall asleep, and one day we shall die to it completely, and a little later the world and mankind will die to it completely, and a little later the world and mankind will die for keeps. And this will not diminish the awesome mystery from which we come, and which beckons us as we return.

And a rabbi who lived on the brink in Nazi Germany told me that at such times doing your duty with a sense of humour is more vital than ever for yourself and others. What was it like, I asked him, in 1938 when jobs were forbidden for Jews? Well, he said, it was like this. A circus came to town offering a hundred marks to anyone who would enter a cage with a roaring lion. A Jew, thinking his death would at least provide for his family, volunteered.

As he gazed at the cruel beast, he shut his eyes and recited the prayers for the dying: 'Hear, O Israel, the Lord is our God, the Lord is One.'

The lion responded: 'Blessed is His name whose glorious kingdom is forever and ever.'

The Jew opened his eyes in amazement as the lion continued, 'Quieten down, grandad. You aren't the only Jew in Germany who is trying to earn a living.'

The rabbis said long ago that this world was not our home or final destination. It was more like a waiting-room or corridor. But it is in a persecution or in a hospital waiting-room, or even waiting for a train that doesn't come, that you need a kindness or a joke the most.

And then, one drizzling night sitting in a station bar up north while waiting for a train, you hear a conversation like this.

'What music would you like me to play?' said the barmaid.

'Play Ayda,' replied her customers.

'You mean *Aïda*,' she said, lifting her glass of Guinness genteelly with a crooked finger.

'No,' he said. 'Ayda, you wid de stars in your eyes.'

And when you hear it you fall about with laughter, and want to hug people. The world is finite but there is some fun in it, if you have no illusions about it.

THIRTY

Anger Is Too Easy

I should like to make it clear straightaway that the things which annoy me most about organised religion and religious people apply to me too. In fact, when I think about the tricks religious people play on God, each other and on themselves, I don't have to go very far. I blush with embarrassment as I think of all the little tricks I got up to, when I was a young rabbi, very insecure and putting on the style.

I get angry with organised religion because part of it is genuine, and part of it is a con trick. Part of it genuinely tries to bring God closer, but another part of it makes quite sure that He is kept firmly away, at arm's length where He can't cause too much trouble.

But my anger starts to evaporate as I realise that organised religion only gives us what we really want – a God, yes, but a tamed domesticated one. I suppose we would like to keep Him like a pet. But when the pet is a nuisance we just tell it to shut up. Yes, I am angry, but I am angry with myself too.

All sorts of people come to religious institutions who don't fit the system and we don't do very well by them – couples in mixed marriages, couples without marriage, awkward people who ask awkward questions, gay people and divorced people. You know, nasty old men and cradle-snatching women have been given a rough time by the godly. We immediately want to judge them and direct them, not to understand them.

Religion has a habit of cheating. Yes, it does seek truth on the highest level, but it is not very good on the lower slopes of honesty. It doesn't start from where people are – which is difficult. It prefers to tell them where they should be, which is a cinch. It cheats on its homework like any naughty child and never spells out how they can get from where they are to where they ought to be – and that makes me very cross.

In a pulpit you can't be answered back – well, you can, but it takes a very brave congregant to do it – and because you are standing above the congregation, not among them, you get illusions of grandeur, and you become pompous, and instead of religion making you bigger you make God smaller and the whole thing turns into an ego trip, and God becomes just another parish-size idol or something for people to emote about. By the way, this is not something imposed on people by a wicked clergy. It's what they want. It's a mutual conspiracy.

I think religious institutions make God so partial. He is made to practise such awful favouritism. There is one set of standards for your own little group, but quite another for everybody else. And so He becomes a totem figure. You manipulate Him and He manipulates you. The one thing I cannot stand is when religion is perverted so that it makes people smaller than they are, and doesn't help them to become bigger in their sympathies, their kindness and their understanding.

A lot of religion is not just worthless: it is positively harmful. It stunts our growth. Just because the word 'religion' or 'God' is used on the headed notepaper doesn't mean that He is in anything of what is written. It could be a fraud, which in any other business would be an offence under the Trade Descriptions Act.

You certainly have to be as subtle as a serpent if you want to keep your integrity in official religion. There is the trick of making the services so long and wordy that God is not allowed to get a word in edgeways. There is the trick of making pious practices feed the neurotic bits of yourself, often with clerical approval. Instead of opening you up to infinity, they become compulsions like not treading on the cracks between paving stones or obsessively touching things.

The most dreadful thing about Religion with a capital R is the way it talks about love but makes people indifferent to others or hate them. There is some good religion in Northern Ireland and the Middle East, but there is an awful lot of sick stuff which finds it easier to erect walls than to build bridges.

I've enjoyed this opportunity to grouse, but one of the most despicable religious attitudes is righteous indignation, especially when you enjoy it. And blow me, I've fallen into it hook, line and sinker. I've enjoyed my anger, but I get angry with myself for being angry. The devil, after all, isn't someone else – it's only that bit of yourself or your own world you can't love.

THIRTY-ONE

Testimony of an Unbelieving Jew

Not long ago I watched some TV programmes on the evidence for Jesus. And though I'm not a specialist in the New Testament, not even a Christian – only an unbelieving Jew – I should like to add my own contribution.

I visited a monastery many years ago at Easter. There was an awful misunderstanding. I was a Marxist fleeing from an unhappy love affair, and wanted quiet. The people at the monastery thought I was coming to be baptised and this was very gratifying for them at such a time. When I arrived I was greeted with enthusiasm. They told me excitedly that there was a retired Bishop of Borneo (surely sent by Providence!) hidden in their cells, who could do the necessary in spite of my advanced years. Now being an obliging, but insecure, person I have always found it difficult to say no to people who seem to know their own mind. Their liturgy overwhelmed me, and I thought, who knows, I might have more talent for divine love than the human sort. I wondered if it was possible to become a monk without becoming a Christian.

But though I teetered on the edge, I never fell into the font because a number of things happened rather quickly. My mother telephoned and said my conversion would take place over her dead body – and my father's too, she added for good measure. My mother is a determined lady. Then the Borneo bishop – whom I had never met – seemed to take against me, and refused to receive me into anything. Why, I still don't know, but I'm grateful.

I'm grateful because you have to believe a lot to be a Christian, and I am not good at it. I come to belief slowly, and with me a little has to go a long way. I get spiritual indigestion easily. And realistically you need a lot more belief to convert than to stay where you are.

There's a story of a Jewish man who was hit by a tram. A kind priest rushed over to him and bent down and asked, 'Do you believe in the Father, Son and Holy Ghost?'

The Jew looked up and said, 'I'm dying and he's asking me riddles!'

Now a lot of Christianity is a riddle if you are outside it. Honestly speaking, it wasn't comfortable in the monastery chapel listening to what the gospels have to say about the Pharisees and the Jews, and I had to remind myself that everybody in the story – except Pontius Pilate, thank God – was Jewish, good, bad and indifferent. And for Jews such things as the Virgin Birth, or the gift of tongues, or the validity of Anglican orders, remain riddles.

But my mistaken visit moved me deeply and it changed my life. This brush with Christianity turned me to God and, because of it, I decided to rediscover my own religion and eventually became a rabbi. My testimony to Christianity is therefore not archaeological or historical or theological – as in TV programmes – it is just personal. The Christian monks made eternity very real to me, because they lived in it. Ever since, I have known eternity is my home, the source I come from, the companion voice inside me, and my destination. They taught me to see the invisible.

I cannot speak about the Incarnation, but I have

witnessed goodness incarnating itself in some Christians I know. Like Rembrandt, I can see it in their faces. It is very attractive. I also cannot speak of the Resurrection, but I have witnessed a new layer of soul forming in them – a kind of rebirth.

I still drop into monasteries and look forward to my first sniff of their distinctive odour. It is an institutional smell made up of strong tea, incense, fish and furniture polish. But for me it is the odour of sanctity, because I always associate it with the rediscovery of my soul.

THIRTY-TWO

By the Platforms of Euston I Sat Down and Wept

It takes two to tango in human love, and with divine love it's no different. It's not just a case of you doing your thing, it's also a case of the Almighty doing His (or Her) thing, and unless you synchronise you get

nowhere. People come and complain, 'Rabbi, I went to the synagogue service, I said all the right prayers, I didn't even walk out during the sermon and what happened – nothing.' They obviously want to swear at you know Whom, but feel a bit uncertain, and just bottle up their crossness and take it out on their family instead.

It happens to me, too. I make an appointment to meet God at eleven o'clock on a Saturday morning in such-and-such a place of worship. I arrive early. I say all the right things, I stand up, sit down and stand up again. I bow here, I bow there and bow-wow in all the right places, but I don't wow Him, because He (or She) doesn't show up, and I'm left holding a prayer book talking to nobody.

Over the years, I've got used to God having a will of His own, which I don't understand, and now I wait to see what He does next. I took a service recently, and it was like talking to thin air. I got through it mechanically, and after smiling toothsomely at the congregation like an American dentist's advert, I went off to meet a friend at Euston Station.

By the platforms of Euston, I sat down (when I could find a seat) and nearly wept, because to crown it all I was early and the train was late. Some rowdy football supporters were wandering around the station with cans of beer, unsure of themselves in a strange city. They knew they weren't wanted. They were defiant and insecure and troublesome. The feeling in the seats was hostile, but the lady next to me looked at them and said, 'Oh the poor luvs, it's a pity we can't do anything for them.' For them she couldn't, but for me she could, because the God I had been hunting through the liturgy peeped out in her compassion. It was our first real meeting that day. In railway stations people are honest. They are worried about their luggage, about their seat, and they are very human. And because they allow themselves to be themselves God is allowed to be Himself (or of course Herself).

While I was sitting on the bench in the railway station, I remembered again this very Jewish story about expectations, which I started telling you and never finished. In this version (there are others) it can be told, and it may provide some more food for thought.

Two Jewish women went for a safari holiday in Africa. As they were going through the bush a great gorilla leaped out at them. One of them managed to get away, but the gorilla grabbed the other and embraced her. And he took her back to his cave and embraced her again. A few days later a rescue party came and she was put in hospital suffering from shock. The other woman, who had made her way back to civilisation, visited her in hospital. She sat by her bed and asked 'But how do you feel?'

Her friend replied, 'How should I feel – he doesn't ring, he doesn't write,' she sighed, 'no grapes.'

THIRTY-THREE

What's in a Name?

My own name is a mess, but I'm stuck with it. My father said I was called Lionel after his grandfather, who was a Lion of Judah no less in fact than in name – a pious toughie who traded horses down the Volga. But my mother said I was Lionel because she had gone to the pictures and seen a Lionel Barrymore film just before I was born, and it was the only nice thing that happened to her in the slump. The Blue bit is what remains of a long East European original, which I shan't tell you because it is unspellable and unpronounceable, with far too many consonants and not enough vowels. And my only namesake in English history is Lionel, Duke of Clarence, of whom I know nothing except that I confuse him with another Duke of Clarence who was drowned in a barrel of malmsey, which must have been a sickly sort of death as it tastes like ecclesiastical wine. And although his end is interesting, it is not inspiring enough to qualify as a Thought for the Day. And was he pushed, I wonder, or just a medieval wino?

But what's in a name, after all? What's the great British public going to make of all those sneaky continental names when it prepares for the elections to the European Parliament? I worked on the continent once, and this is my humble guide.

'Christian' is not quite what you think. It can mean fellow-travelling Stalinist or fascist. It can mean cautious conservatives, or the equivalent of the SDP at prayer, or just that Jews are not admitted. 'Democratic' is favoured by authoritarian establishments and strong-minded terrorists. 'Liberal' is used by sober-suited stockbrokers and the debris left over from the last student revolt but one. As 'Socialist' is used by *everybody*, far right, right, left and centre, it should be treated as an old-time piety, or a politeness like 'esquire'. And the best of British luck to our electors as they fortify themselves with fish and chips and vinegar before they make their choice.

In the Bible names are important. Jacob, for example, changes his name and his character after an angel gives him a good kick up the thigh. No, I'm not making it up, you can find it for yourself in Genesis Chapter 32, verse 28, as I recall. In institutional religion lots of the names and labels don't mean nearly so much, and it's better to trust your own judgment as you hack your way through the ecclesiastical undergrowth. Follow the good advice in the psalm: 'Taste and see that the Lord is good.' Also remember the words of the gospels: 'By their fruits ye shall know them.' These are very good tests.

Not long ago I was with some religious novices, and I had a taste of true religion and real goodness and holiness which was quite unmistakable. Once you've been given the fresh milk of human kindness the canned sort just won't do.

Nationalism is, of course, much more dodgy than religion because its catchwords are often only beguiling labels, which on examination, after you have emoted, have no real sense or content in them at all. And this sort of froth can get you into trouble.

There was a Jewish guy who saw a Far-Eastern gentleman in a city restaurant. He was out of sorts, so he picked up a plate of noodles (as one does when one feels like that) and he poured it over the Chinese gentleman. 'That's for Pearl Harbor,' he said.

'But I'm Chinese, not Japanese,' said the oriental. 'Chinese, Siamese, Japanese, what's in a name?' said the Jew.

As he went to pay his bill, the Chinese gentleman suddenly hit the Jewish guy over the head with a salami. 'That,' he said courteously, 'is for the sinking of the *Titanic*.' 'But,' shouted the Jew, 'the *Titanic* was sunk by an iceberg!'

'Greenberg, Goldberg, iceberg, what's in a name?'

THIRTY-FOUR

Blues in the Night

A lady wrote to me. She enjoyed my Thoughts for the Day, she said, especially the jokes. She was going through a crisis and sometimes couldn't sleep – just lay there waiting for sleep to come, which it didn't, just a fitful doze which came too late. Anyway, the jokes cheered her up, and they cheer me up too, for like lots of people I also suffer from occasional bouts of depression and anxiety.

If they happen in the night, I wouldn't stay in bed – or bother about counting sheep, or feeling life isn't fair. Of course it isn't fair – that's obvious – but even

a depressive can make the best of it. Some people have an odd reaction to this situation. They feel guilty because they can't sleep – religious people especially have to remind themselves that religion isn't there to produce guilt, but kindness. When I first caught religion I used to feel guilty because I didn't feel guilty, and then got scruples and felt more guilty than ever.

So when you get downstairs try to be kind to yourself – love yourself a little. If you want to cry, why not? Tears don't run down your cheek for nothing, and somewhere on the way you must have got hurt. Don't think of your failures, but of your successes. After all, you're here, aren't you? You've survived. Congratulations!

But actions speak louder than words, so love yourself with something. I love myself with a ¼lb of whole nut chocolate for depression, and a ½lb bar for anxieties. Now treat yourself to some milk of human kindness: you can provide your own. Beat together one raw egg, ¾ pint of chilled milk, a few drops of vanilla, 3 tablespoons of sugar and a grating of nutmeg. You have to stop crying, or your tears will make the milk salty.

You've been told many times about loving your neighbour, but the Bible text is not as simple as that. You should love your neighbour as you love yourself, is what it says. So be charitable to yourself as well – it's a command. Of course you've made mistakes – that's what living is about. Yes, of course you've sinned, but religion is meant for people who fall down and pick themselves up.

Now, sitting back in your chair, you can try some contemplation. Play with it. Don't take it too heavy – St Teresa didn't always, so why should you? Just watch some clouds of unknowing drifting by. Work out if you're in the third or the fourth mansion of the Interior Castle or just stuck in the castle moat – that's more interesting than sheep, isn't it? Your night of the soul may be dark, but it doesn't have to be dreary. The world isn't fair, as I've said, but there is something to be redeemed in every situation and in every person in it – no matter how unpromising. That's faith, which we all live by in impossible situations – like this one, for example.

At a funeral a Jewish minister has to tell the truth about the deceased, but he also has to say some good thing about him. Occasionally this proves very, very difficult. A minister who had to bury a real scoundrel consulted a more experienced colleague. But even he could not help him. The dead man was that nasty. 'You will just have to wait for inspiration,' he said. Well, the funeral started and the sermon began, and the mourners waited expectantly.

'He wasn't exactly pious,' said the minister unhappily, 'and he didn't really have any friends. His wife isn't here because she died of grief, and his daughter isn't here either because after he turned her out she walked the streets. His son doesn't speak to him. . . .' He paused and began again. 'His parents also didn't answer my letter, and you can understand it, as he gave his mother a heart attack.'

The minister paused again, and then inspiration came and his face lit up. 'But compared to his brother he was a saint!'

No, don't take it personally, as you'll get depressed all over again and then you'll get too fat, which really *is* depressing.

THIRTY-FIVE

Plump and Juicy

As a child I was blessed twice every morning, once at home and once at school.

Everything my family did was excessive, for they combined Slav 'intensity' with Jewish 'heart'. My grandmother never knew pain, she only experienced 'egony – egony'. Some of my relations believed in the Kingdom of God, others beavered away for the republic of goodness. Alas, their zeal outran their discretion: some disappeared, and some died for causes that were not equal to their sincerity.

Emotional blackmail was used with gusto. My grandfather clutched me and raised his eyes to heaven. 'Lord God of Israel,' he intoned, while my granny keened away in the kitchen, 'spare this child who shames his family in the eyes of Israel.' This was for adding too much rum to my lemon tea. Sometimes my treachery was raised to the national level. 'O God of our fathers, show mercy unto this child who shames us in the eyes of the Gentiles.' This was for running up and down stairs. Knowing I was loved, I never took this nonsense too seriously.

My morning blessing meant more to me. My grandfather clutched me to his midriff, and juicily asked

God to bless me during the day. He didn't go in for short measure, and I still remember the comforting phrases, 'Spread the tabernacle of Thy peace over him. . . . May the angels and archangels stand at his right hand, and at his left.' This comprehensive insurance was certified by my grandmother, who moaned 'Amen, Amen' from the kitchen, as each clause was specified. Sometimes when it got too fruity we all burst into giggles. It was the only 'ham' allowed into the household.

At English school my blessing wasn't like that. Life was real, and life was earnest, and it certainly wasn't a joking matter. If I was well-behaved, an ethical deity would bless me from a distant heaven. It was very sincere and well-meant, but there were no giggles and no rum.

Occasionally ministers of religion, when they bid me farewell, adjure me to 'take care', and then they jump an octave into the thinnest and purest of spiritual heights and add, 'Bless you – bless you!' They mean well, and I am truly grateful for their blessing – indeed I am grateful for any I can get, but I think of grandpa and granny, and their 'hamming it up' (you should pardon the expression), and decide I prefer my blessings plump.

THIRTY-SIX

A Blessing for Bad Times

She was a very irritating lady, and I didn't like her – I still don't. I am relieved that lots of other people feel the same. My fellow-Jews certainly don't like her, for though she came from a pleasant and cultured Jewish family, she neither understood Judaism nor liked it. Some of her writings are so prejudiced that I threw one of her books out of the window.

She wobbled on the edge of the Catholic church for years, but never fell into the font, so Christians just have to put up with her, because they don't know where to put her either. I heard she had the same effect on Trotsky, whom she hid for a night in Paris. I am pleased she irritated everybody, irrespective of race, religion or creed.

Her life was short and her wartime death in London both tragic and embarrassing. She only allowed herself the rations of Occupied France, and so starved herself into death. Was her death a true sacrifice, or a wilful martyrdom, or anorexia nervosa, or was she just off her oats? Who knows?

But I can't put Simone Weil aside. For Malcolm Muggeridge, Mother Teresa represented absolute love, but Simone Weil represented absolute truth.

Now truth is not comfortable. It doesn't warm you, like generosity, or make you glow, like piety. Religious people play fast and loose with it, because it doesn't suit their book, sacred or secular. 'The truth,' say the gospels, 'will make you free.' But who wants that? It doesn't make you cosy.

I first encountered Simone Weil when I decided to study for the rabbinate, and was very greedy for the consolations of religion. Some, like silence, were licit; most were not. I enjoyed titles, ritual and dressing-up because I was insecure. I got a kick out of chatting to the cosmos, and felt I was on to a good thing. But since then my religion has turned inside out. How hard true religion is. How dark and devastating are its truths. How much dying is implicit in eternal life!

It is a giving, not a taking. Prayer is not changing the universe, but working to change oneself. What we get and what we expect from life are not the same. As any child can tell you – it's not fair, God doesn't play cricket. Devotion means recognising God in bad times and in events which seem to destroy us. If you can look into this blackness, and are heroic or foolish enough to try and trust it, then you will turn to Simone Weil, like me.

In Jewish prayer books there are pages of blessings for perfumes, people and other pleasantnesses. But the crunch comes towards the end. It says curtly – 'A blessing to be said on hearing bad news – Blessed are You, Lord, the judge of truth.' It is a pity Simone Weil was so prejudiced about the religion of her birth, for it was exactly what she taught.

THIRTY-SEVEN

God Called on Me

Prayers I make out of necessity and prayers I recite out of duty require little formal preparation from me, but the prayer which is a privilege is another matter. There is one great difference between them. In the first two I called on God, because I had to or because I was paid to – in the last God called on me, and this meant I had to take a step sideways, out of my normal life, to meet Him.

This means I must make an empty space in a busy life. I have to postpone appointments, make arrangements with my secretary, and dictate my unfinished business. A holy day and a holiday are not that different, with the same mixture of anticipation and worry. I have to get away. I cannot have this meeting at home, for there is no empty space there. The rooms are too crowded with memories and anxieties. The windows jammed long ago, and no gusts of fresh air can blow away the trivialities of my life.

I am apprehensive, too, about the meeting. I am anxious lest nothing should happen, and even more anxious in case something should happen. An empty space in my life is uncomfortable and I want to fill it in. But this emptiness inside myself is necessary, so that I can free myself and be my true self for the meeting. To do so, I have to clear away a lot of inner junk. Some of it is secular junk, and some of it is religious junk.

The first is fairly easy to spot – 'I'm all right, Jack', 'The grass is always greener', the distortions of the rat race, and more concern for my own image in other people's minds than God's image in me. I am afraid that if I get rid of all my false images, there would be nothing of me left.

The religious junk is more difficult to spot. I start by talking too much, praying too much, trying to be too good. The sentiment isn't mine, so the language isn't either. I get tripped up by the 'thees' and 'thous' and 'ests' and 'eths'. I finally say 'To hell with it!' and begin again, less effusively.

I start again, but this time I make God too chatty. I am a ventriloquist, and He is my dummy. I know exactly what He has to say. I learned it all in a seminary, and as I passed my exams, I can't be wrong, or rather He can't, or rather I . . . . Anyway, I pray for God's presence, and my divine dummy says rather ambiguously, 'I'm yours.' And once again the only real word I utter is 'Damn!'

And then I know I've had it, and look forlornly round the alien room, but something begins to sing in the emptiness, and it is my privilege to listen.

THIRTY-EIGHT

The Great Unblessed

As I was driving down the road with an Irish friend, we passed a church with a modern bell tower. At the top was a belfry made of iron bars. 'By God,' said my friend. 'Sure, they've done it at last! 'Tis what they've always wanted. They've caged the Almighty.' He brooded a moment and then shook his fist at the offending structure and shouted: 'But He won't endure it. He'll never let them get away with it. He'll get even with the boyos yet. . . .' etc., etc.

Now institutional religion (I call it 'Religion with a big R') is like a box. If you like the idea of a religious box, then you call the box a shrine or a reliquary – if you don't, you call it a God-cage. When I decided to study for the rabbinate, I liked the idea of living with others in a religious box. Inside we might be droopy, but we would at least be pure. It would provide a foretaste of the communion of saints and the life of the world to come. But I found a seminary wasn't a box, it was more like a boxing ring, a mirror reflecting all life, sacred and profane, in it.

Because I was an adolescent with pimples, I got disillusioned and decided to leave religion and go to hell in my own way. I would be a devil, I thought, and say 'No' to God and 'Yes' to anything anybody should ever ask me, if they asked me, which was more than I dared hope.

And that period of my life was quite exciting, because I met people who cohabited, lived together and paired off in quite extraordinary combinations and sequences. My puzzle was that they didn't seem to get much pleasure out of it. I listened as they anguished, analysed and agonised over their interesting state. 'Well,' I thought, 'a Jewish suburban marriage should be like a rest cure after this!'

For though my new friends thought they lived outside God, I knew God lived inside them. I saw His fingerprints on their lives. Though they thought they were the great unblessed without any benefit of clergy, their lives glittered with undisciplined acts of generosity and love. In fact they continued my religious education, teaching me the same truths as my seminary, but with different illustrations.

I learned again that God is everywhere. He resides

in Arks and on altars, as any worshipper knows through experience. But if you seek Him, you find Him, in boardrooms and bedrooms, in Hymns Ancient or in Juke-box Modern, in discos or pubs. In God, distinctions between rich and poor, slave and free, Jew and Greek, or German or Arab for that matter, don't matter. You can learn this from the spirituality of Paul, or it can be deduced from the lowest common denominator of human experience – a shared hangover.

I learned that God is my eternal home – He is not my life sentence in gaol. So why do we try to limit God? It is because He is so vast, and the distance that separates us so daunting. We get tired of straining upwards so that He can reach us. We cop out and try to make Him smaller and lower, so that we can reach Him – a deity just the right height for a cage or a kennel. But the world shows us how foolish that is. My liturgy asks a great question: 'Where is the place of God's glory?' I understood afresh the answer. 'Blessed is the Lord, whose glory is revealed in every place!'

THIRTY-NINE

Something for Nothing

My grandfather used to say you get nothing for nothing, and some rabbi once said you shouldn't go to a doctor who charges nothing because his services may be worth nothing. As a child I used to wonder if I could ever find a way to get the chocolate out of the slot without putting my penny in. Well, actually you can sometimes do it with chocolate, because a disreputable school crony of mine did exactly that, but you can't do it with blessings, as I found out much later. They don't just drift in like smoke or lust; they have to be struggled for, and you earn them as you earn your living. Look at Jacob, who cheated his own brother Esau out of his birthright and then met him by accident many years later. The night before he met him, he didn't just moon about. He struggled with his angel so hard that he ruptured himself in the thigh, though I don't understand how, before he got his blessing.

This is how it was with me. I had played the stock market because I had more greed than sense, and lost nearly two thousand pounds. The money rankled and I couldn't get it out of my mind. Somehow I couldn't let go of my losses. I was glued to my own failure and disappointment. It is odd how lots of people are imprisoned, not in their memories of triumph and success, but by bitterness and anger from the past.

I had a lot of work to do and pushed the whole affair from my mind. The Jewish High Holydays were coming on and I had to work out five sermons with different endings and yards of liturgy complicated by the traditional feuding of rabbi, cantor and choir. I also had to think out Hebrew prayers, English prayers, choral inserts and memorial prayers for the dead. But every time I sat down to think about any of them, all that came into my mind was my lost two thousand pounds. It wasn't the money that worried me, because like most Jews I am not a mean person, but it was my pride that was hurt. I just wasn't as clever as I thought.

I thought about a sermon on the Holy Spirit, and it became 'The Holy Spirit and my two thousand'. In desperation I decided to give the traditional Jewish sermon on family life, but that turned into 'Jewish family life and my two thousand'. So one day I sat in an empty synagogue, and wondered what I could offer God to get my blessing. What do you give a being who has everything? And a voice spoke inside me and it said, 'The only thing I want from you is your failure. Your losses are the only genuine things you have to offer.' I struggled like Jacob and wrestled in prayer, and then I said magnanimously to God, 'Take it! I make You a present of the two thousand pounds I lost. I give it to You.'

And God said 'Thank you very much', and I got my blessing, for I produced a lovely sermon on Jewish family life, about which I have little experience, and a touching one on the education of Jewish children, about which I have no experience at all because I haven't got any. It wasn't exactly something for nothing, but it was a close thing.

FORTY

Pickles and Piety

I never wanted to be a fireman or an engine driver, and when I was given fire engines or Meccano sets I stacked them away in a cupboard until I learned to recycle them. I must have been a precocious child because I wanted to be a high-powered lawyer and make love to Shirley Temple. As regards both ambitions I have been an under-achiever, or perhaps non-starter would be more accurate.

Instead I became a rabbi, which puzzled both my family and myself. My mother said I did it to spite her and my father, and there certainly was an aggressive twist to it, because for some years my poor father had to eat forbidden food in the bedroom, not to offend my piety. With the years my mother's puzzlement has increased. 'Why,' she says, 'if you have to be a rabbi, must you be the only one who writes a cookery column for a Christian paper?'

'Why, indeed, do I mix pickles and piety?' I brooded. And I knew the answer straightaway. It was my grandmother, God rest her soul, who mixed food and faith so well in my belly and my being, that I have never been able to separate them since.

Her parents were killed in a Russian pogrom. So her village clubbed together and bought her a steerage ticket to England, where it was rumoured she had a rich uncle who ate chicken and sat in a parlour wearing a gold watch. She was an orphan of about nine, so they put a label round her neck giving her name, and the possible name of her possible uncle. On the boat she met my future grandfather, who was not much older, making his way to America from the Tsar's army. When they arrived, the two children were given soup at the London docks, and they clung to each other for some years, and eventually set up home together.

For some years my grandfather thought this was America. My grandmother couldn't work it out, and retired to her kitchen where she cooked enormous pots of soup, ladling it out to penniless Yiddish poets, Irish immigrants and miracle rabbis, who couldn't perform the miracle of a decent meal for themselves.

All the while I, as a child, sat on the boiler by the steaming pots and listened to my grandmother's commentary on the human condition. Every Thursday night she woke me, and together we dropped little parcels of food or money through the letter-boxes in our block, to homes where there was illness or no job, so they could celebrate the Jewish Sabbath which was the birthday of creation. We went out at night to spare them the shame of charity. She never had a proper holiday. But once a year she looked up rooms to let in high-class areas like Golders Green or Hampstead and together we visited them, not because she could ever dream of taking them but because she wanted a glimpse into the life of rich people who ate smoked salmon, unafraid of bailiffs or pawnshops.

A Catholic friend of mine took me to a mass, and when I heard the words of invitation to the Lord's supper I thought of her, and said the memorial prayers for her under my breath. Because of her I understand why Christians experience God's presence on their tongues, and Jewish rabbis in the Middle Ages asked for their coffins to be made out of the holy planks of their kitchen tables, presumably leaving their widows bereft of holy husbands and cooking space.

'Blessed are You, Lord our God, king of the Universe, who feeds the whole world.' Just like granny, in fact!

FORTY-ONE

What the Rabbi Gave to the Bishop

Many years ago I quarrelled with a friend, and it's taken me years to get over the grudge. But God moves in a mysterious way, and this is how He got me moving. It happened via a birthday, a bishop and a

purloined lily. I can tell the story now, to my shame, because the principals in it are all dead except me.

I had arrived at a station on the continent to attend a meeting of Jews, Christians and Moslems. The Christians in their nice Christian way thought that if we knew each other, we would love each other. Unfortuately the Jews wanted to know the Moslems, but the Moslems preferred to be matey with the Christians, and the Christians pursued the Jews, so that limited our progress.

But to get back to the lily. A breathless cleric at the station explained that it was the bishop's birthday and wafted me and a bemused Moslem to the bishop's palace. We stood in a long line of people greeting the bishop. They all bore presents. You know the sort of thing one gives – a second-hand Rembrandt, a medieval embroidered cope, a family heirloom or hot-house blossoms from your own greenhouse. And after they were presented they were placed against a wall. Alone in the queue, my Moslem colleague and

I had nothing to offer – like two of the three wise men who had failed in their duty. It was embarrassing, and our cleric looked thoughtful. Suddenly he darted to the line of presents and came back with two lilies, lifted from one of the baskets near the wall. 'Give the bishop one each,' he hissed. The Moslem looked grim holding his blossom, and I looked furtive holding mine. Both of us were built more like Oscar Wilde than the Blessed Damozel.

When we got to the bishop, our guide said fulsomely, 'Here is Rabbi Blue and he brings you a Jewish lily, and here is Mr So-and-So who brings you a Moslem lily!' I tried to get away quickly from the scene of the crime, but to my horror the bishop burst into tears and said he had never had a present like it – and this was quite untrue, because he had received the same lilies now twice over.

Reporters and photographers were summoned and they clicked away while I wondered if I would be discovered and end up as a terrible example in an anti-semitic paper. My Moslem friend was trying, as well he might, to figure out if it was all a plot of the CIA or the KGB or MI5 or the Israelis, or all together in league with the lily-growers and Pre-Raphaelites.

But now for the grudge. I was just going back to the continent for another conference. I sat in a synagogue trying to think about the meeting, but my mind kept drifting back to the bishop and the stolen lily. Well, I couldn't do anything about it now. Then my mind started rabbiting back to my grudge, to the friend I mentioned, and suddenly it dawned on me how God wanted me to tie them up. This time I would give that nice bishop, now dead, a real present. I would write a letter of apology to my former friend and make him, the bishop, a present of a good deed done in his name. I did manage to write the letter – just – because I had promised it to the bishop in my prayers. Wherever the bishop now is, I hope he enjoys it as much as more normal gifts like talc, aftershave, Rembrandts, hankies, copes and chocolate. But these, as you will appreciate, may be inappropriate to his situation.

Now you probably know what the actress said to the bishop. Well, if you don't by now, I certainly can't tell you – especially in a spiritual context. But now at least you know what the rabbi gave to the bishop. And as my old friend, who has now received the letter, said when I told him the story, 'The ways of God are kinda weird.' And that's quite enough tangled uplift for now.

albert